Vegetable Growing

Keith Mossman

Edited for U.S. Gardeners
By Marjorie Dietz

Pocket Gardener

Floraprint

Published 1977 by Floraprint Limited,
Park Road, Calverton, Nottingham.
Designed and produced for Floraprint by
Intercontinental Book Productions
Copyright © 1977 Intercontinental Book Productions
and Floraprint Limited. North American edition
Copyright © 1981 Intercontinental Book Productions and
Floraprint U.S.A.

ISBN 0-938804-09-X

Design by Design Practitioners Limited

Photographs supplied by Floraprint Limited (copyright
I.G.A.), Suttons Seeds

Printed in U.S.A.

Contents

1 Garden tools and equipment   4
2 Soils and digging   6
3 Fertilizing your garden   8
4 Planning your own vegetable plot 10
5 Sowing and planting   12
6 Caring for growing crops   14
7 Watering and mulching   16
8 Harvesting and storage   17
9 Tents and frames   18
10 Pests and diseases   20
11 The vegetable garden month by month 22
12 Cabbage family (brassicas)   26
13 Peas and beans   34
14 Permanent crops   39
15 Salad crops   41
16 Root crops   48
17 Miscellaneous crops   57
   Index   64

1 Gardening tools and equipment

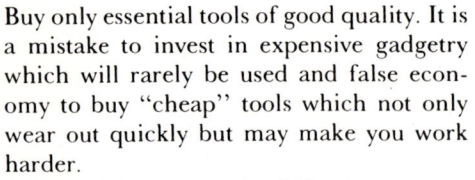

Buy only essential tools of good quality. It is a mistake to invest in expensive gadgetry which will rarely be used and false economy to buy "cheap" tools which not only wear out quickly but may make you work harder.

Essential tools are the following:

A trowel and garden line
A sharp-pointed stainless steel trowel is the most useful of small tools. It is handy for making planting holes, for lifting plants from the seed bed and sometimes for hand weeding. Keep a spool of nylon line handy for marking rows. It will not deteriorate in inclement weather, therefore able to be used again.

Dutch hoe and draw hoe
The Dutch hoe is used for surface cultivation and the destruction of weeds. To use it, you walk backwards and make short forward strokes. Several types are available. The draw hoe is also used for weed control and is especially good where weeds are thick or root systems are deep. You can walk forward or backwards when using this hoe, depending on which method is most comfortable. To ease cultivation with either hoe, keep the blade sharp.

Digging fork and spade
These should be stainless steel, which has long life and makes the working of moist and heavy clay soils much easier. Wooden handles should be ash. Handles are made in different lengths so you should select one that suits your height. It is not necessary to buy full-size tools. A small spade may not dig as deeply, but will probably make the work quicker and less tiring.

Garden rake
This is essential for smoothing the soil surface of your garden prior to sowing or setting out started plants. Debris, such as stones and weeds, also are easily removed. Tough steel teeth break up large clods of dirt.

To this basic equipment you will probably find it necessary to add other items, but it is wise to buy only those for which you discover a real need in your own garden. Likely purchases will be the following:

A wheelbarrow
Select a model that rolls easily and is well-balanced. The bed should have ample capacity and be constructed of heavy-gauge steel.

A watering can with detachable nozzle. This can be used not only for watering, but for the application of liquid fertilizers. An extra can should be kept for applying weedkillers and used for no other purpose.

A length of plastic hose. Select a hose of large enough diameter to do the job required and made of a material that will not become stiff with age. Fit your hose with a spray nozzle that adjusts from a heavy single stream to a fine spray.

Rotatillers

The rotary cultivator is a valuable power tool for vegetable gardeners. It is used for deep and surface cultivation, greatly reducing time and labor spent digging and hoeing. Rotatillers have blades rotating around a horizontal axis, driven by a gasoline engine and capable of being adjusted to work at varying depths.

Some machines have large driving wheels with the rotor mounted at the rear. Others are pulled forward by the front-mounted rotors.

Units pulled forward by rotors are generally less expensive than those that have rear-mounted driving wheels. They also are most widely used in small-medium size plots. Because the rear-mounted models are less fatiguing, these are best for large gardens. They also are more versatile, as many have snowblades and other attachments.

2 Soils and digging

Before you can grow anything the soil has to be cultivated, and different soils need different treatment. The gardener has to understand and make the best of his soil, because although it can always be improved its basic character cannot be changed.

Types of soil

Heavy or clay soils These are wet and sticky in winter, drying to hard clods or a cracked surface in summer if wrongly treated.

Dig early in winter, exposing a rough surface to frost, which shatters the clods into a fine tilth ready for sowing in spring. Work in bulky organic manures when digging. Never tread on the soil when it is wet. If the soil should be waterlogged when you wish to dig, try spreading some peat on top. This will make digging easier and save you getting embedded in mud.

Sandy or light soils These are easy to work, warm up quickly in spring and so are good for early crops. They dry out in summer and are often poor because plant food is quickly washed out.

Dig in moisture-holding material – manure, compost or peat. Apply complete fertilizers shortly before sowing. During the growing season top dress with fertilizers and water them in, or apply liquid fertilizers. Mulch with peat or compost.

Loams These are generally fertile soils, lighter than clays but holding moisture better than sands. A good loam has a naturally high humus content and when it derives from, for instance, old pasture-land, it should support crops well for several years with little manure or fertilizer. But if you are lucky enough to have such a soil you should treat it generously from the start, otherwise the initial fertility will be lost and take years to rebuild.

Alkaline soils Often grayish in color, these dry quickly after heavy rain. This natural drainage makes for an early start in spring, but alkaline soils need the same attention to watering and mulching to keep crops growing in summer.

Alkaline soils rarely need lime and benefit from all the organic manure and peat that you can give them. Crops such as potatoes, which dislike an alkaline soil, do much better if plenty of peat is worked into the planting site.

Get to know your soil and the way it is affected by differing weather conditions. In a new district, learn about its peculiarities from gardening neighbors.

If certain crops fail persistently, change varieties, substituting those likely to suit the soil better: stump-rooted carrots for long varieties on clay soils, for instance, or snap beans on sandy loams.

Drainage: to improve waterlogged soil, construct a soakaway. Dig a hole about 3 ft (1 m) deep, fill with hard-core topped by gravel, and replace topsoil.

1. Place one foot – left or right – on a shoulder of the blade and drive it *vertically* into the ground using just the weight of the body. If you drive it in at an angle the digging will be less effective.

2. Pull the spade handle back to lever the chunk of soil loose, lift it with one hand well down the shaft at the point of balance.

3. Throw it gently forwards, twisting the spade slightly so it slips from the blade. Repeat this in a steady rhythm. When you reach the far side of the plot walk back and begin another row.

The why and how of digging

Digging is the first and most important part of cultivation. It breaks up the soil so that the surface weathers into a friable tilth in which seeds can be sown, it allows the penetration of water and air, both necessary for the health of soil and plants, and it permits the removal of weeds and the incorporation of manure and compost.

Digging is the hardest physical work in the gardening routine, but at the right tempo and in reasonable stints it need not be tiring. Start at a left-hand corner of the plot to be dug and work from left to right. Use a spade rather than a fork unless the soil is hard to penetrate, and dig only when the surface is fairly dry or lightly frozen.

Pick out all perennial weed roots and consign them to the bonfire. Annual weeds may be buried if completely covered, but are best taken to the compost heap.

Right: basic soil preparation. In plain digging the spade goes one spit deep and the soil is thrown forward, leaving only a narrow trench. In double digging a wider trench is first taken out and the subsoil is dug with a fork. The first trench is then filled with soil from the second, and so on, the first soil excavated being barrowed to the end of the plot and used to fill the last trench. In ridging the soil is thrown forward to form a ridge-and-furrow pattern, exposing it to frost and improving drainage.

Plain digging

Double digging

Ridging

3 Fertilizing your garden

Soil fertility must be replenished after each crop is harvested. This means you must put back major plant foods, nitrogen, phosphorus and potash, along with any trace elements such as iron, zinc and copper.

Organic and inorganic fertilizers are available to help build back your soil's plant food content. Organic types include various manures, stems and stalks plowed under from the previous year's garden, dried sewerage, yard/kitchen compost, spent brewery hops, worm castings and spent mushroom compost.

In addition to resupplying plant foods to the soil, organic fertilizers contribute to tilth. Soil does not crust over, allowing air and water to enter the root zone. Humus-rich soil particles hold onto minute amounts of moisture and food, rather than allowing them to move deeper into the earth before being used. In this environment, micro-organisms are allowed to grow, breaking down complex plant foods to a form plants can use.

Inorganic fertilizers are chemical compounds that carry a given percentage of each major plant food. A 50-pound bag of fertilizer with an 8-4-4 analysis will contain 4 pounds of nitrogen and 2 pounds each of phosphorus and potash. Balance of the bag's content is an inert carrier that aids application.

Both types of plant food sources have their place in the gardener's fertility program. It is wise to dig in organic fertilizer in late fall or early spring. A soil test can then be made. Kits are available for determining soil fertility from local garden centers. Also check with your county extension agent to see whether your state Land Grant University will make such tests.

So your test is accurate, take samples from various parts of your garden. Once test results are available, you can apply chemical fertilizer at the recommended rate two weeks prior to sowing or planting. Occasional supplemental feedings should be made during the growing season. Use inorganic fertilizers. They are easy to apply accurately and most forms of nitrogen, phosphorus and potassium in them are available immediately to stimulate growth.

Organic Fertilizers

Of the many organic fertilizers mentioned

Nitrogen
Essential to the growth of leaf and stem. Lack of nitrogen produces weak growth and pale-colored foliage.

Phosphorus
Promotes germination and root growth. Vital to the maturing plant and the formation of fruit and seeds. Phosphorus shortage reduces crops of peas, beans other seeds and fruits.

Potash
Necessary to plant health and the ripening of fruit. Improves resistance to disease. Light soils are most prone to be deficient in potash.

These three major plant foods are contained in most fertilizers. Select a bag analysis that contains liberal amounts of all three for vegetable crops.

Making a compost heap

Compost may be made in heaps or containers. The heap for an average garden should measure 4 x 6 ft., but space should be allowed for two heaps so you can keep replenishing your supply. Build your heap on soil, not on a solid base. Start with vegetative waste spread to a height of 1 ft. Sprinkle with sulfate of ammonia or a commercial activator and water it in. Add a thin layer of soil and another 1 ft. layer of waste, and sprinkle this with garden lime and more soil. Then add another layer of waste and more activator. When the heap is 4 ft. high, leave it for several weeks, then turn it onto the adjoining space, watering the material where dry and covering with a layer of soil. Leave it until the compost becomes a uniformly brown color. A home-made two compartment wood bin is a good container. Small manufactured units also are available. Follow manufacturers' instructions.

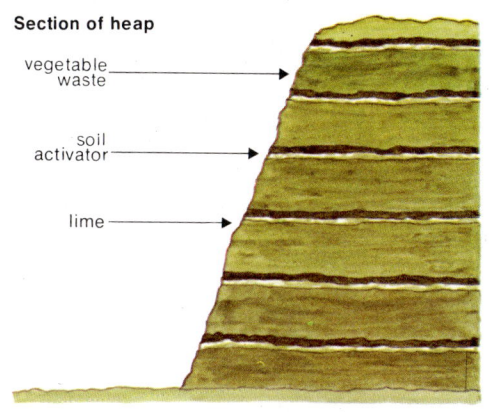

Section of heap

vegetable waste
soil activator
lime

Heap sinks rapidly during construction.

Two-bay compost bin with front of one section removed for access.

in this chapter's introduction, two kinds are most widely used by U.S. gardeners:
1. Manure from farms and stables.
2. Compost from a heap started on the gardener's property.

Farmers regularly sell or give away manure. If you are not sure who to contact, check the classified pages of your local newspaper.

Manures are also available in bagged form. These have been dried and are sold at nursery, hardware and supermarket outlets.

However, homemade compost is the cheapest of organic foods and is easy to make. The idea is to return to the soil all available vegetable waste in a suitable form. Materials include annual weeds, crop residues, lawn mowings and soft hedge clippings ... even kitchen vegetable scraps.

A complete step-by-step guide for establishing your own compost heap is shown on Page 9. If you do not wish to build your own containment area, there are a number of compost bins available commercially.

Soil Amendments

Soil amendments are those materials that do not add nutritive value to the soil, but which promote a suitable growing environment. These should be incorporated into the soil prior to planting your crop. Which soil amendments are added, however, depend upon the character of soil in your garden. If your soil has a heavy clay content, making spading or cultivation difficult, you will want to add peatmoss and sand. Peatmoss and heavy amounts of organic fertilizer also are helpful amendments when worked into sandy soils because food and water stays in the root zone longer.

Most gardens require lime every 3-4 years. Because fertilizers make the soil acidic, lime is required to bring soil pH readings back to a neutral position. If you are just starting a new garden, remember that grassland soils probably do not need lime before planting, although those that were formed under forests, have been wet, or created by volcanic action, probably do.

Regardless of soil type, check for lime requirements when testing soil fertility levels.

4 Planning your vegetable plot

Make the most of your vegetable garden by planning ahead. The easy and obvious course is not always the best in the long run.

Give the vegetables the most open position possible, cutting back tall hedges on the south and west sides. Avoid sites overshadowed by trees. A few dwarf fruit trees can be included in the larger home vegetable garden, since they cast little shade.

Try to arrange things so that the crop rows run north-south, giving equal sunlight on both sides of a row and reducing the extent to which short crops are overshadowed by taller ones. Remember that good paths between beds and to the garden shed and compost heaps make for ease of working. The grass path is the worst, having to be mown and trimmed in the summer while in winter it becomes bare and muddy. One of the best and most quickly laid is that made of cement paving slabs with non-slip surface. Kitchen garden paths need not be more than 24 in (60 cm) wide.

Planning the crops

Decide at the start of the season on the crops to be grown and the space to be allotted to each, otherwise you may realize too late that some varieties you particularly wanted have been crowded out.

Crop rotation The object of 'rotating' crops is to ensure that the same crop, or a similar type of crop, does not occupy the same ground year after year, which encourages the build-up of pests and diseases and depletes the soil of particular nutrients. Divide the vegetable plot into three roughly equal areas or beds and the crops into three groups, growing each group in a different bed over a three-year period. The groups are roots (including potatoes), brassicas (all the cabbage tribe) and miscellaneous, which includes peas and beans.

The manurial treatment of the groups is different: the brassicas should receive most of the organic manure and the miscellaneous crops any left over. Root crops are not manured. All the beds get fertilizer dressings before sowing or planting. It is not, of course, possible to keep to the rotation in every detail. There is always some overlapping, and quick-growing crops such as lettuce and spinach may be fitted in wherever space is available.

Successional crops

Achieving maximum yields from your garden depends on making the fullest use of the ground. This does not mean cramming rows and plants closer together than the recommended distances, which often means a lower total yield, but ensuring that that group is not left unused or cluttered with the remains of a previous crop.

Wherever possible follow a main crop with a successional one, usually quick-maturing and harvested the same season, sometimes the following spring. Clear away the old crop immediately it finishes, and lightly fork over or rototill the surface. Most successional crops are started in the summer, when everything must be done to conserve soil moisture. Don't dig deeply, because this releases moisture and brings up intractable clods. Leave the roots of early pea and bean crops in the ground, to release the nitrogen accumulated from the atmosphere in the root nodules. Just hoe the topsoil. Work in a complete fertilizer at 1½ oz per sq yd (50 g per sq m), water drills thoroughly in dry weather before sowing, and keep germinating seeds and young plants watered until well established. Follow broad beans and early peas with broccoli, snap or lima beans, or summer squash.

Catch crops Some vegetables with a short growing season can be 'slotted in' between other crops to make the most of the ground. Radishes can be sown together with slow germinating seeds such as parsnips.

Three-year rotation

First year

Bed A Root crops

No manure dug in. Apply complete fertilizer before sowing. Use peat moss freely when planting potatoes on alkaline soils.

Root crops
Potato, carrot, parsnip, rutabaga, turnip, beet, salsify, onion (bulb), Jerusalem artichoke, shallot.

Bed B Miscellaneous crops

Some manure if available. Fertilizer before sowing. Peas and beans fix atmospheric nitrogen in their roots and leave the soil richer in this element.

Miscellaneous crops
Pea (all varieties), bean (all varieties), spinach, sweet corn, squash, celery, leek, all salads, including salad onions, tomatoes and cucumbers.

Bed C Brassica crops

Dig in as much manure as possible during winter. Lime after digging if necessary. Fertilizer before planting.

Brassicas
Brussels sprout, cabbage, cauliflower, broccoli, kale.

Second year

Bed A Misc. crops
Treat as Bed B, first year.

Bed B Brassica crops
Treat as Bed C, first year.

Bed C Root crops
Treat as Bed A, first year.

Third year

Bed A Brassica crops
Treat as Bed C, first year.

Bed B Root crops
Treat as Bed A, first year.

Bed C Misc. crops
Treat as Bed B, first year.

Final distance between:

	plants	rows
Potato	24 in (60 cm)	12 in (30 cm)
Carrot	9–12 in (23–30 cm)	4 in (10 cm)
Onion	12 in (30 cm)	4 in (10 cm)
Beet	12 in (30 cm)	4 in (10 cm)
Squash	2½ ft (75 cm)	2½ ft (75 cm)
Broad bean	24 in (60 cm)	6 in (15 cm)
Sweet corn	18 in (45 cm)	12 in (30 cm)
Leek	18 in (45 cm)	9 in (23 cm)
Tomato	36 cm (90 cm)	18 in (45 cm)
Celery	9 in (22 cm)	9 in (22 cm) (self-blanching)
Cabbage	24 in (60 cm)	18 in (45 cm)
Broccoli	24 in (60 cm)	18 in (45 cm)
Kale	24 in (60 cm)	18 in (45 cm)

5 Sowing and planting

Buying seeds

Obtain catalogs and send in your seed order very early in the year. Latecomers are apt to find the varieties they want out of stock. Seedsmen usually specify an average length of row or number of plants to be expected per packet of seeds, and quantities ordered may be based on your plans for the season.

Buying plants

Some vegetables are transplanted to their final quarters and not sown where they are to grow. If you intend to buy plants rather than raise them yourself, it pays to get the best obtainable, preferably from a local nurseryman. Avoid brassica plants that are leggy and drawn from crowding in the seed-bed, long-stemmed tomato plants with bluish foliage, and yellowing squashes. The best plant is not the largest, but the one in vigorous growth, short-jointed, with leaves of a healthy green.

Left: stocky, leafy cabbage plant grown in seed-bed with plenty of room.
Right: leggy plant grown in overcrowded row.

Seeds and sowing

Seeds in sealed vacuum packs may be kept for a year after the packeting date if the packs are unopened. In ordinary packets, brassica seeds remain viable for several years but the germination of others cannot be relied on after a year. Sowing defective seed means losing irreplaceable time.

Conditions for sowing To germinate, a seed must have moisture, warmth and air. The temperature must not be too low, the soil must be in the right condition, and the seed not sown too deeply.

Recommended sowing dates are only approximate and vary from region to region. Do not begin the first sowings of the year until the soil starts to warm up and signs of growth are evident.

Soil preparation Lightly fork in a pre-sowing fertilizer dressing about a fortnight before starting to sow. If the surface, left rough after winter digging, is dry enough to walk on without soil sticking to your boots, rake it down to a fine, crumbly tilth. If still wet, wait until just before you are actually ready to sow.

Rake the seed-bed in both directions, to ensure the soil is well broken up.

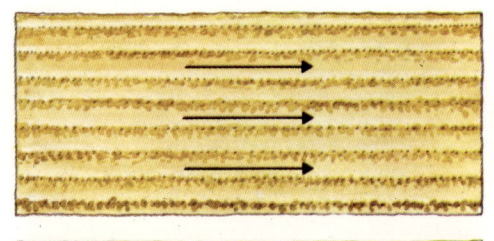

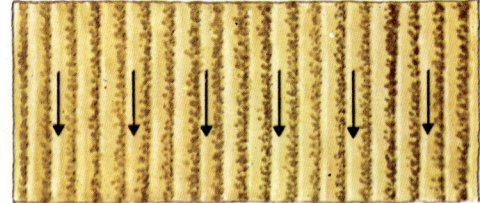

Sowing

To make a drill, put the garden line in position and make sure it is taut. With the draw hoe, make a shallow furrow, guided by the line. For small seeds, make the drill V-shaped with the corner of the hoe blade; for large ones, such as peas and beans, take out a wide flat-bottomed drill with the full width of the blade. Measure the distance to the next row and move the line.

To sow small seeds such as lettuce or carrot, tip some from the packet into the palm of the hand and deposit them evenly and fairly thinly along the drill from between thumb and forefinger. Beans are placed individually but peas may be scattered liberally (but not touching) in a wide drill.

Pelleted seeds, which are made larger by being covered with a protective coating, are all spaced individually to facilitate thinning.

Cover the seeds by pulling the soil into the drill with the hoe or the back of the rake, leaving the surface level. Tamp it down gently with the flat of the hoe blade or by *light* pressure of the foot.

In dry weather water the drill thoroughly before sowing and continue to water until emergence of the seedlings. Moisture is absolutely vital, and pelleted seed especially may fail if the seed-bed dries out for a short period. As a general rule, early sowings are covered less deeply than those made later in the season. In the first case the soil is warmer just below the surface, in later sowings moisture is conserved better around the seeds by placing them a little deeper.

Planting out

For planting out tender subjects such as tomatoes and squash choose a warm spell when all possible danger of late frosts is past. Unless you can protect with Hotkaps nothing is gained by being too early.

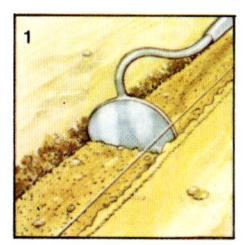

Water pot- and flat-grown plants an hour before planting. Brassica and similar plants grown in a seed-bed should be well-watered the day before planting out and lifted with the trowel, ensuring that plenty of soil clings to the roots. Make planting holes with the trowel, setting all types of plant a little deeper than they had been growing previously. Firm the soil, making sure that the roots are not left in a cavity at the bottom of the hole. Water after planting and keep watered until established and growing.

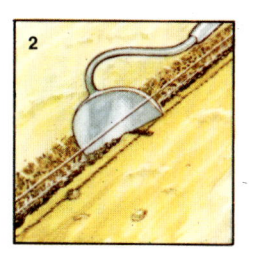

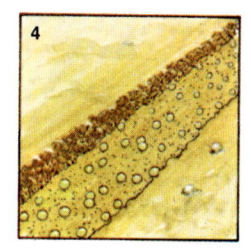

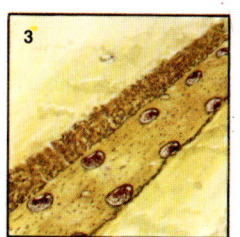

Types of drill

1. Wide drill, made with full width of draw hoe.
2. Narrow drill, made with corner of hoe blade. Used for all small seeds.
3. Beans in staggered double row in wide drill.
4. Peas scattered liberally (not too close) in wide drill.

Firm the soil with flat of hoe blade (or light foot pressure). Water seedlings when transplanting and continue until they are established.

Use a trowel rather than a dibber and make the hole large enough to take roots easily.

Plant with the lower leaves just clear of the surface and no bare stem showing.

Plants in peat pots are planted pot and all, the top of the pot being just covered.

6 Caring for growing crops

Thinning

Plants growing in a row must have enough room to develop properly. If crowded together, normal growth is impossible; if too far apart, space is wasted and the row yields less than its potential. There is therefore an optimum distance for best results.

Plants raised in a seed-bed or cold frame are planted at their final distances in the row, any thinning being done at the seedling stage in the seed-bed. Peas and beans are spaced when sowing and are not thinned. Pelleted seeds are spaced about 1 in (2·5 cm) apart and subsequent thinning is easy. Early and adequate thinning is most necessary in sowings of small seeds, which invariably come up too thickly.

Thin in three stages. First, as soon as the seedlings are large enough to handle, to about 1 in (2·5 cm) then to double this distance as the seedlings grow, and then to the final distance for the crop to mature. Never thin to the final distance in one operation; a few seedlings are always lost from pests or climatic conditions and if this happens after thinning to the full distance the row will be depleted and 'gappy'. Also, if seedlings are allowed to grow between thinning stages the thinnings in some crops will be of usable size and will not be wasted. Among root crops, small carrots and golf-ball-size turnips and beets are pulled as required while the rest of the crop is left to reach full size. Spinach seedlings of a fair size are usable if the roots are trimmed off and the thinnings of lettuce are a salad ingredient long before the plants have heads.

Thin only when the soil is moist, to minimize root disturbance of the remaining plants. In dry weather give a good soaking the day before thinning: the work is easier if the tops of the seedlings are dry. Patience is needed to 'single' the crop, to reduce each clump of seedlings to one plant, but this is essential. Beet is especially difficult because each 'seed' is really a fruit containing several seeds, but monogerm seed producing only one plant per seed is now becoming available.

Weed control

This is a vital part of cultivation. Weeds compete with the crop for moisture and nutrients and, if allowed to get out of hand,

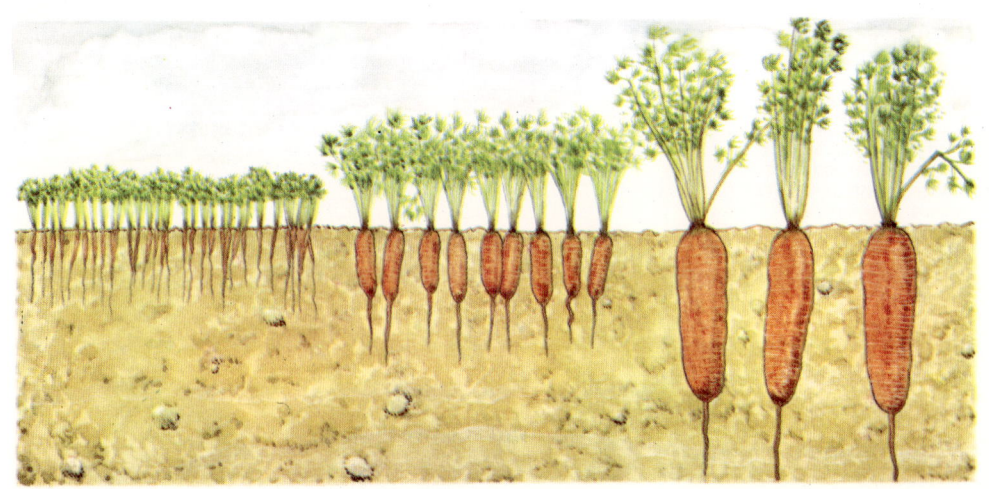

1. Carrots after initial thinning, still crowded.

2. After second thinning: every other one now removed for use.

3. Carrots growing on to full size after final thinning.

Types of hoe: The draw hoe (*left*) is drawn towards the operator, who moves forwards. The Dutch hoe is pushed away from the operator, who walks backwards avoiding ground already hoed.

A contact herbicide may be used on weeds between crop rows. It should be applied with a can and sprinkler bar and should be held close to the ground to avoid splashing crop foliage.

may smother it completely. Deal with them before they become a menace.

Hoeing and hand-weeding Hoe between rows regularly when the surface is dry. Do it even if no weeds are visible and you will destroy weed seedlings before they appear. Keep the hoe blade just below the surface and do not chop or jab close to the row. A rototiller may be used with the blades set very high, provided there is sufficient inter-row space and room to turn at the headlands without damage to the crop. Remove weeds to the compost heap if rain is likely or the small ones may re-root.

Weeds actually growing among crop rows must be pulled up by hand with as little disturbance to the crop as possible. Large weeds with a strong root system should be eased out of the row with a trowel. Hand weeding is essential for close set crops where other methods could damage plants and weeds alike.

Weedkillers Both state and federal authorities are becoming increasingly critical of chemical weedkillers, and especially their use by non-professional gardeners. Most home owners today would do well to stick to the hoe as a means of eliminating weeds or the lazy gardener can apply a mulch (see page 48), which has the additional benefit of contributing humus to the soil as it decays.

If you have a large garden and wish to try using chemical weedkillers, here are a few that are not yet restricted: Dacthal, a herbicide applied to the soil before weed seeds germinate, which can be used with many vegetable crops; Dymid or Enide, and Vegiben, all used as above. Always follow directions on the container.

Using weedkillers
Your local garden center and your county extension agent have information on which chemical weedkillers are licensed for use in your state.
Follow directions on the container *exactly* to avoid injury to yourself, to adjacent plants and to the environment in general.
Mix only enough for immediate use. Store out of children's reach and *never* put surplus solution in soft-drink bottles.

7 Watering and mulching

The soil is a reservoir in which the rains of winter are stored for use in the growing season. The better cultivated it is, the more spongy humus it contains, the greater its water-holding capacity and the more accessible is the moisture to the plant roots.

Soak drills thoroughly before sowing in dry weather. Continue to water until germination.

Conserve moisture by spreading 3 in (7·5 cm) of mulch along both sides of crop row.

Water intake
1. When fully grown, the plant takes much more moisture from the soil than is lost by direct evaporation from the surface.
2. Repeated small waterings only moisten the top of the soil and do not reach the feeding roots, which may be attracted upwards as a result.
3. Well-cultivated soil encourages a good root system which collects more moisture.
4. A subsoil broken up during digging permits moisture to be drawn up from deeper levels.

In the summer, moisture is lost faster than the rainfall can replace it, partly by evaporation from the surface but even more by plants transpiring from their leaves the water taken up by their roots. Crops in full growth are the ones most likely to need additional supplies of water.

How much water? It is worse than useless to give little drops in dry weather. You cannot slightly moisten the soil all the way down, for water penetrates to the dry soil below only when the upper layers are saturated. Inadequate watering causes the roots to spread upwards to the saturated layer, where they are more vulnerable to the inevitable periods of drying out.

Average summer rainfall is from 2 to 3 in (5 to 7·5 cm) per month, and in a dry spell moisture reserves are quickly used up and the crop begins to suffer. Remember that 2 in (5 cm) of rain is the sort of quantity needed to be effective after a few weeks of summer drought.

Crops that respond most to watering are early potatoes and carrots, lettuce, spinach, squashes, peas and snap beans. Whether you water by watering-can, hose or sprinkler, give an adequate quantity to a limited area at each watering rather than a little to every crop.

Mulches A mulch is a layer of organic material such as peat, compost or well-rotted manure applied to the soil to reduce moisture loss by evaporation. It should be spread to a depth of 2 in (5 cm) on both sides of the row when the crop is past the seedling stage and the soil is thoroughly moist. As an alternative, black polyethylene sheet may be used, which also suppresses weeds. Simplest of all is the soil mulch, the layer of loose topsoil created by regular hoeing, which prevents moisture being drawn to the surface.

8 Harvesting and storage

Harvesting at the right time is an important factor in the quality of vegetables and sometimes in the size of the crop. Many vegetables can be stored in the freezer, and for successful freezing they must be harvested in perfect condition and at the right stage of growth. The advice that follows is, however, concerned only with harvesting for immediate use and storing those vegetables that keep without freezing.

Potatoes
Earlies are dug as required and the shorter the time between digging and cooking the better the flavor. Dig later crops when the tops have died down and the skin of the tubers has set and cannot be rubbed off. Avoid damage when lifting. Store in a cool but frost-free place in complete darkness. Frost destroys the tubers and light turns them green and renders them inedible.

Turnips and rutabagas
Lift in October or November and store in a cool place. A few degrees of frost will not hurt them. Green top turnips are very hardy and may be left in the ground for much of the winter, any not used producing edible tops for greens when growth starts in spring.

All root crops should be stored as clean as possible, soil being rubbed off without damaging the skin.

Carrots and beets
Pull young roots during the growing season. Lift for storage in October, remove tops (twisting off rather than cutting beet tops), and store in boxes covered with slightly moist sand or peat.

Parsnips
Leave in the ground and dig as required, but lift remainder of crop in spring before they start new growth.

Squashes
Butternut squashes, pumpkins and winter squashes keep for several months if well ripened. Leave them on the plant until the skin is absolutely hard and sounds like wood when tapped. Store where they are safe from frost and inspect frequently for signs of deterioration.

Onions
Lift when growth finishes and dry very thoroughly spread out in shed. Hang up in nets or tied in bunches in a dry, airy and frost-free place. The chief enemies of long storage are warmth and dampness. Shallots are stored in the same way but are usually harvested much earlier than onions.

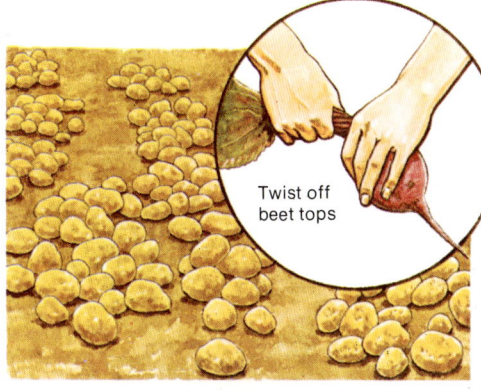

Twist off beet tops

Potatoes spread out for drying

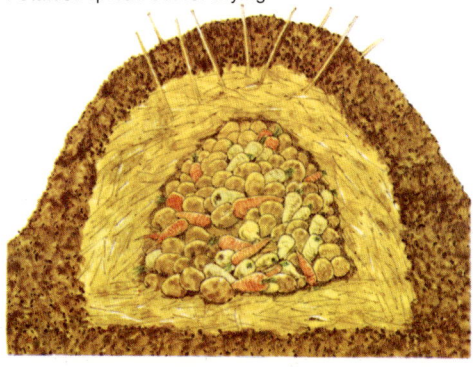

Making an onion rope

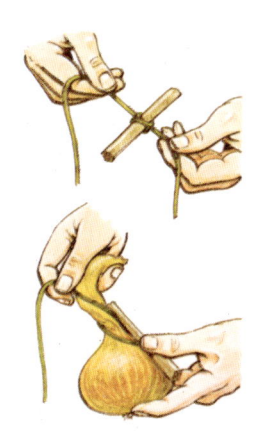

Left: clamps are used for storing beets, carrots or potatoes.

Ropes of onions are attractive, space-saving and easy to make, as the above diagrams show.

9 Tents and frames

Gardeners have traditionally used glass to protect crops from cold weather, in effect, extending the growing season.

The first form of glass protection, and still practiced today, is the use of empty bottles. Inside these bottles, tender young plants are warmed by the sun, benefit from the humid environment maintained inside and are protected from strong winds and frost. Translucent plastic bottles, with the bottoms cut out, are also performing this service.

Other forms of protection have evolved, with many European gardeners employing wire frames containing sheet glass. Popular here in the U.S. are wax paper throwaway protectors. On both sides of the Atlantic, however, the polyethylene tent or tunnel is widely used. These tunnels cover a whole row and are formed by placing wire hoops every three feet, then stretching polyethylene over them.

In the U.S., however, these tunnels are primarily used by commercial growers, particularly in California, to protect winter tomato crops.

These devices can extend the growing season in either fall or spring. Autumn-sown crops such as lettuce benefit greatly. Peas, carrots, beets and radishes get off to a better start in early spring. The gardener can also harvest beans, tomatoes and sweet corn nearly a month earlier than he normally would.

Although techniques for growing specific crops under polyethylene, glass and wax paper tents are mentioned elsewhere in this book, the main factor determining success is the availability of soil moisture. Soil cannot be allowed to dry out.

The garden frame

This device is practical for the hobby gardener, as it can be used to start a large num-

Two forms of the European protective glass frame are shown below. While they do protect plants from wind and frost, they are heavy, making a change of location difficult. Care must also be taken in their handling to avoid glass breakage.

Polyethylene tunnel: Made of polyethylene sheeting stretched over wire hoops. The tunnel has the advantage of cheapness, but needs care in operation.

ber of crops from seed without monopolizing available window light inside the house.

A frame is relatively easy to build, because, all it is, is a solid walled box covered with glass panels.

Depending on how early it is used and climate, the frame can either be heated or not. However, even in mild climates, seed germinates better if the soil is warm.

Heating can be accomplished in one of several ways. Manure, used as a bed under trays or flats, provides a great deal of warmth. Light bulbs can be used to moderate temperatures, particularly at night. Sacking should be placed over the bulbs if there is danger from frost, however.

Commercial growers and serious hobby gardeners agree that the most reliable means of furnishing even heat in a frame is to install a heating cable or mat. A standard 60 ft. cable can be positioned in loops about 8 in. apart to heat a 6 x 6 or 6 x 8 ft. bed.

Regardless of whether your frame is heated or not, a sunny, southern exposure is best. The soil should be well-drained and some protection from wind should be provided from the west and north.

It is a good idea to limit depth of the

Garden frame: Valuable for raising half-hardy vegetable plants such as sweet corn and for growing cucumbers and melons. Give it a sheltered site facing south.

frame to 6 ft., otherwise working with plants inside becomes too strenuous. Glass panels used on top should lift up, so they can be propped to admit ventilation when temperatures get too high inside. Although the frame should be tight, expensive materials are not necessary. The use of old storm windows is a cheap way to provide light required. These can be mounted on hinges attached to the back of the frame. Even if the glass has been broken out, plastic sheeting can be fastened to these frames.

Garden frames are also being offered commercially. Most have clear plastic tops and wood or heavy plastic sidewalls. Although these units are small compared to what can be built at home, there are some useful accessories, which include temperature gauges that automatically open the top of the frame when inside temperatures exceed 72 degrees F.

10 Pests and diseases

Plants have a natural resistance to their insect and fungus enemies. The more vigorous a crop, the less likely it is to be attacked and the quicker to recover.

Health hints

Maintain soil fertility and keep crops growing steadily by watering and cultivation. A stunted plant is the first to suffer infection or insect damage.

Prevent overcrowding of crops by early and adequate thinning and the removal of weeds, which compete for food and moisture, and harbor pests.

Watch over garden hygiene. Trim waste and weedy corners and long grass where slugs take refuge. Clear away remains of crops, especially the stumps of Brussels sprouts and winter cabbages, which carry the cabbage troubles into a new season.

Inspect crops frequently and deal promptly with any trouble. A puff of insecticide today is worth more than a full-scale blitz next week.

Practice crop rotation, i.e. avoid growing similar crops always on the same ground.

Buying and using pesticides

Suitable pesticides may be bought in liquid form to be made up into a solution for use in a sprayer or syringe, but for the small garden the most convenient forms are the aerosol and hand duster.

The safest preparations are those based on pyrethrum and rotenone, both non-toxic to humans and animals and reasonably effective against a wide range of insect pests. Dusting packs containing a combination of pyrethrum and piperonyl butoxide, or aerosols containing pyrethrum and lindane are also perfectly safe, and with one of each you are equipped to deal with most of the pests likely to be encountered.

Precautions in using pesticides
Read the instructions. Note that certain plants such as squashes and cucumbers may be sensitive to the spray. *Never* use household fly-killers on plants. Keep to the recommended time between using the pesticide and harvesting the affected crop. Don't spray young seedlings or flowering crops in strong sunlight – wait until evening.

Common insect pests
Black aphids
Attacks broad beans and occasionally runner beans. Like all aphids, multiplies and spreads very rapidly. Pick out the growing points of broad beans as soon as enough pods have set and spray with malathion as soon as clusters of aphids are noticed. On runner beans they frequently appear first on the flower buds and these should be examined occasionally for any sign of them.

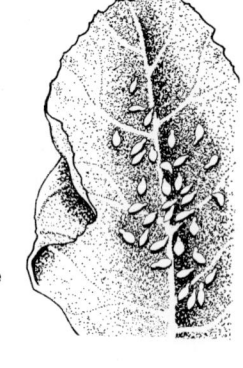

Cabbage aphis
Especially troublesome on cabbages and sprouts if it gets into hearts and other sheltered spots. Look for clusters of grayish insects and spray or dust immediately. In bad cases an aerosol may be ineffective and you should use a syringe and a solution of malathion to penetrate the crevices.

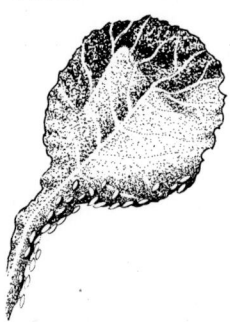

Cabbage caterpillars
The larvae of cabbage white butterflies, these ravenous creatures can be extremely destructive. All brassicas may be affected in summer. Use a pyrethrum dust or Sevin, or *Bacillus thuringiensis* as soon as they are noticed, and repeat the treatment as more hatch out. For a consideration, the children may be persuaded to pick them off by hand and deposit them in a jar of salt water.

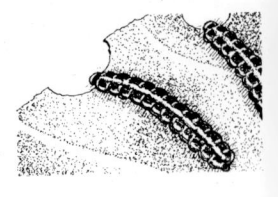

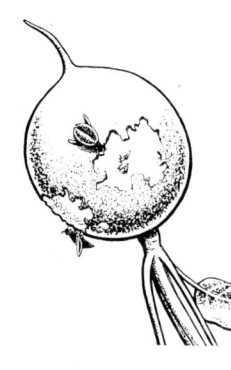

Flea beetle
Very small, punctures and seriously damages seedlings of brassicas, turnips, rutabagas, eggplant and radishes. Keep plants well watered and dust frequently with pyrethrum or rotenone.

Cabbage root fly
The larvae particularly attack cauliflowers, eating into the roots and causing the plant to collapse. Dig up affected plants with nearby soil and burn them. As a preventive, apply diazinon dust round each young plant.

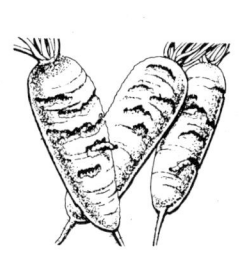

Carrot fly
The insect is attracted by the scent of crushed foliage during thinning, where it will lay its eggs. Use pelleted seed to reduce thinning to a minimum.

Slugs
Use pellets containing metaldehyde under a slightly raised tile to keep them away from birds and pets. Or sink saucers in the soil, and fill them with beer.

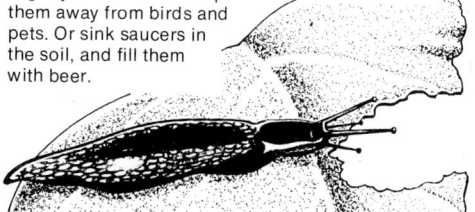

Common diseases

Only two bother most gardeners' crops.

Potato blight
Spray maincrops with Bordeaux mixture or maneb in July if the season is wet. At the end of the season cut off blighted tops and burn before lifting the tubers.

Club root
This disease of the cabbage family can become a serious nuisance. If you see any signs of swollen and distorted roots among brassicas, stop growing them on that piece of ground for two or three years and give it a heavy dose of garden lime after winter digging, followed by a lighter one the next year.

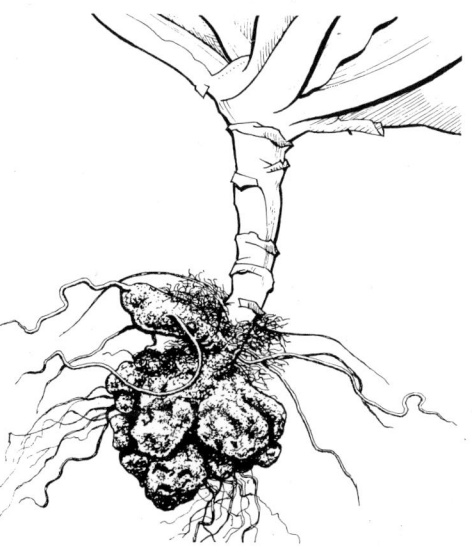

11 The vegetable garden month by month

January

Order seeds, seed potatoes and onion sets, keeping mainly to well-tried varieties, but including a few new ones as well.

In the South and milder climates of the Southwest and Pacific Coast continue clearing spent crops. Begin digging and adding compost if the ground is workable and not too wet. Apply garden lime if a soil test shows it is necessary for the crops to be grown in that space.

Harvest winter greens such as kale. There will also be leeks, and in mild regions Savoy cabbage, Brussels sprouts, spinach and cauliflower. Seakale and chicory forced indoors will be ready now. Dig up Jerusalem artichokes and parsnips as required. If prolonged frost threatens, cover root crops in the ground with layers of newspapers or straw so that lifting still remains possible.

In a heated greenhouse you can now sow onions, leeks, and cauliflowers.

Check over vegetables in storage and throw away any that are beginning to rot.

February

Set up seed potatoes in trays in a light, frost-proof place to sprout.

In the milder, coastal areas of the Northeast, much of the Southwest, Pacific Coast and upper South it may be possible to sow peas and broad (fava) beans.

Toward the end of the month in a sunny window, under fluorescent lights or in a heated greenhouse sow broccoli, cauliflower, celery and cabbage.

In mild climates continue harvesting cabbages, leeks, parsnips, and celery. If the ground was not dug last month, do so now, turning under cover crops and applying lime where necessary. Apply a complete fertilizer, such as 5–10–5 to ground intended for planting in March, but rake it only when the surface is dry. Do not apply lime and fertilizers at the same time.

At the end of the winter it is very important to check vegetables in storage for any that may be rotting. You should also rub sprouts off potatoes in store.

March

Pull up old broccoli, cabbage and Brussels sprouts stalks and spent kale plants. All the brassicas are prone to diseases and can harbor overwintering insects.

Turn under cover crops such as rye sown in the fall.

Throughout this month in most of the North, earlier in milder regions such as New York's Long Island, sow peas, broad beans, spinach, cress (all kinds), roquette, broccoli raab. Toward the end of the month sow radishes and lettuce.

Cold frames need special attention in all areas. Unseasonably warm weather – and quite the reverse – can occur.

Continue to plant onion sets.

If your last frosts should end in about 8 weeks, it's a good time to sow seeds of various tender vegetables, such as tomato, eggplant and pepper indoors.

In the warmest regions of the South and Pacific Coast, outdoor activity is well along with the setting out of such seedlings as tomatoes and eggplants.

April

In much of the North the harvest can start with lettuce from the cold frame or lettuce thinnings from the open ground. When thinning spinach, use the thinnings in salads. Cress sown earlier should be ready. An asparagus bed makes a good place for sowing all the cresses as their shallow roots can't interfere with the deep-rooted asparagus plants. A few radishes, either from a frame or open garden, should be ready; spring onions should also be ready now.

Prepare and plant new asparagus beds. Prepare a place for celery plants to be set out the following month.

Put down bait to combat destructive slugs. Do this especially around lettuce plantings.

Sow sweet corn and snap beans in milder regions. Indoors in the North, sow 1 or 2 seeds per pot of squash, cucumbers, melons in individual peat pots. If a sunny window is lacking, grow under artificial lights. They should be planted outside in about 3–5 weeks.

May

Thin early crops as soon as the seedlings are large enough to handle.

Sow snap beans about the middle of the month in most Northern regions or anywhere as soon as the soil has warmed. Don't rush this if the weather remains cool and wet. Snap beans revel in heat. This same advice holds true for sweet corn. Sow as soon as possible any crop mentioned in two preceding months if first sowing has failed or been delayed by weather, also lettuce and radish for succession. Make first sowings of rutabaga and winter squash for winter use.

Plant tomatoes, peppers and eggplants under Hotkaps or improvised cloches.

Harvest asparagus from established buds, cutting all shoots including thin and deformed ones. Harvest summer cauliflowers, bending leaves over the curd to prevent discoloration by the sun.

Plant celery seedling and water well. Cucumbers and squash can be sown in place.

Hoe regularly and water growing crops in dry weather.

June

Regularly pick peas and broad peas so later pods continue to fill. If you find your pea harvest is ready all at once, you may want to plant one of the less commercial varieties next time that ripens its pods more gradually. In New England and other cool-summer regions, another pea sowing is possible. Plant the variety Wando.

Sow squash and cucumber seeds; continue to set out tomatoes, eggplants and peppers (under Hotkaps in the far North if weather remains cool and wet). Sow all beans except broad – bush and pole snap beans and bush and pole limas. If space is limited, choose the pole types.

In some regions the two-month harvest of asparagus is close to final cutting to allow ferny top growth to develop and build up roots for next year's crop. Sprinkle a complete fertilizer such as 5–10–5 over the bed toward the end of the month and if the soil is dry, water it in.

Mulch all crops with compost, pine needles, rotted manure, best applied on wet ground.

July

Remove the growing points of staked beans when they reach the tops of the poles.

Stake and tie tall-growing tomatoes and rub out sideshoots as soon as they are seen. Earth up the stems of potatoes to keep upright.

Keep a close watch on maturing vegetables such as green beans. Gather them while young and in top condition for immediate use or freezing. A few days too long in hot weather can make a serious difference to quality. Early tomatoes that may be ready include Early Salad, Early Girl, Springset, Presto, and Small Fry. Also ready are cucumbers, zucchini and other summer squashes, globe artichokes and early potatoes.

For harvesting this fall sow quick-maturing endive and snap beans. Make further late sowings of spinach, carrots, lettuce and winter radishes.

Make final plantings of kale and broccoli, doing all you can by careful planting and watering to establish quickly.

Watch for pests, especially worms. Dust with rotenone or Sevin.

August

Bend over the tops of fully grown onions to encourage ripening of the bulbs. Harvest shallots, breaking up the clusters and storing when dry.

In mild climates sow cabbage, spinach, onions, broccoli for winter and spring harvesting. In most Northern regions it is still not too late to sow radishes and quick-growing lettuce for autumn use. The lettuce can be left in the open ground where the fall season is long and mild. In colder areas transplant seedlings into a cold frame.

Gather runner beans before the pods swell with developing seeds; once seeds are allowed to form the plants cease to produce. In hot weather they may need picking every two days. Sweet corn should be tested by squeezing kernels and using before contents are solid and starchy. Use or freeze cobs as soon as possible after harvesting, as conversion from sugar to starch continues.

Start earthing up celery that needs blanching at the end of the month.

Lift and store unused early potatoes as the tops die down.

September

Cut off and burn potato tops infected with blight. If the skins of the tubers are set lift them immediately; if not, leave them for another week or two until the skins are too tough to be easily damaged in lifting.

Pull up tomato plants with unripe fruit if frost seems likely, hanging them under cover for ripening to continue.

Complete harvesting of squashes, cucumbers and broccoli. Lift onions and garlic and dry thoroughly before storing. Pickling onions will be ready for harvesting.

There will also be cauliflower, the ever-present cabbages, self-blanching celery, and the first Brussels sprouts and savoy cabbages.

Transplant seedlings of cabbage and other crops for winter harvesting in mild climates. Continue to transplant lettuce sown last month in frames.

Cover late-sown snap beans with tunnels of polyethylene stretched over wire frames to prolong cropping.

Earth up celery for the second time, leeks for the first.

October

Harvest and store all root crops for the winter: carrots, beets, rutabagas, turnips, and winter radishes. Handle beets carefully when lifting. Left in the ground and pulled as required are Jerusalem artichokes, parsnips, celeriac, horseradish, and possibly turnips.

Complete earthing up of trench celery and leeks. Start forcing chicory and blanching endive. Cut down asparagus 'fern' when it turns yellow and lightly earth up the bed or row. Mulch with manure or compost.

Continue picking Brussels sprouts, which will be improving in quality, and remove dead leaves from the plants. Do not on any account take out the tops. Remove dead foliage from seakale and cut down the stems of Jerusalem artichokes to keep them from being blown down.

Sow winter cover crops such as cereal rye, if this wasn't done last month. The grass will make an attractive 'lawn' for the vegetable garden during the dreary months and will continue growing even under snow. In spring the rye can be spaded over to supply humus to the soil.

November

Complete lifting of all root crops to be stored under cover. If very wet and dirty, spread them out in a shed to dry and rub off soil before storing.

There are still many other vegetables to take from the garden, including blanched celery, leeks, Jerusalem artichokes, cauliflower, Brussels sprouts and cabbages. The first blanched endive and forced chicory will also be ready; lift all remaining chicory roots and seakale to force as desired.

Clear away remains of spent crops. Take the yellowing leaves off Brussels sprouts, heel over cauliflowers to protect them from frost, and put a layer of straw over the crowns of globe artichokes.

Press ahead with winter digging whenever the ground is fit to work and not planted to a cover crop. Do not try to dig when the soil is so wet that it clogs on your boots. That does more harm than good and makes the work harder. Manure for next year's peas, beans, onions, leeks, celery, and spinach.

December

This is the month for general garden maintenance – for tidying up after the preceding year's work and preparing for the next growing season.

Keep a check on cold frames if they contain lettuce sown earlier in the fall. This year you will still have celery, leeks, Jerusalem artichokes, cabbages, parsnips, and broccoli from the garden, as well as blanched endive and forced chicory – if you planned carefully!

There will also be many root crops stored indoors, including potatoes, onions, turnips, carrots, rutabagas, and beets. Keep them in a frost-free, warm place.

Make sure overwintering crops like globe artichokes are protected with straw over their crowns.

Place manure and compost in convenient heaps in the garden for use in spring.

Cover compost heaps with soil and add additional material such as leaves.

Order catalogs for new season unless already on their mailing lists.

12 Cabbage family (brassica crops)

Brussels sprouts

One of the hardiest and most valuable of winter greens. Two rows of sprouts, say about thirty plants, will yield good weekly pickings from fall to early winter.

Soil
Like all the cabbage family, sprouts are fairly greedy, but only moderate amounts of manure or compost should be dug in during the winter. Over-feeding tends to produce lush, leafy growth which suffers in severe weather, and too many 'blown' or open sprouts. The crop often does well on land manured the previous season, provided any lime deficiency is corrected and digging is done early to allow the soil to settle. Loose ground produces poor sprouts. Rake in 3 oz per sq yd (100 g per sq m) of a general fertilizer when leveling the site for planting.

When to sow and plant
Not too early in most Northern areas with hot summers, since the sprouts should begin to form in the fall during cool weather. Best time is late spring to early summer.

How to sow and plant
Plants are sometimes available from local outlets in the spring. Or start from seeds. Sow in a seed-bed in the open or sow thinly in drills ½–¾ in (2 cm) deep and 6 in (15 cm) apart, and thin to about 1 in (2·5 cm) apart as soon as possible. When about 3 in (7·5 cm) high, lift carefully with a trowel after watering and plant out 24 in (60 cm) each way. Water in and keep watered until established.

Right: Tight, medium-sized sprouts of the type preferred for kitchen and freezer. Loose, 'blown' sprouts often result from loose, over-manured soil.

Above: Well-filled stem of Brussels sprouts. Pick them from the base so that the upper sprouts will develop.

Below: Plant seedlings out at 24 in (60 cm) intervals.

Time to germination
10–14 days. Germination is good, and if pelleted seed is used, it may be safely spaced at almost the final seed-bed distance.

Season of use
Fall to early winter.

Good varieties
The best variety for the home garden is Jade Cross Hybrid. Second to that is Long Island Improved.

Special note
Avoid those commercial varieties in which all the sprouts develop simultaneously. Pick systematically, taking the larger sprouts from the lower part of the stem and removing the top only when crop is finishing.

Tomatoes in window boxes or small containers require watering two or three times a day in hot weather.

Growing Vegetables in Containers

Although gardening in containers is covered in much greater detail in our book *Balcony, Patio & Window Box Gardening*, some mention of this practice should be made here.

First of all, it does not matter whether you are living in a house with limited planting opportunities, an apartment or condominium, you can harvest a surprising volume of vegetables by gardening in containers.

Seed producers around the world have developed a large number of compact growing varieties that produce well in patio pots, tubs, hanging baskets, window boxes and a host of receptacles that may not be in use around your home.

The main criteria for these planters is that they hold soil and that there is some way for excess water to drain. Containers used will vary with household. Some of the more unusual successfully cropped include wash pails, eaves troughs, old tires, cement blocks and coaster wagons.

Besides producing mouth-watering salads, and baked dishes, container crops can lend a festive mood to a patio or balcony because lush green foliage grown by many varieties provides a pleasing contrast with red or yellow fruit.

For instance, several cherry tomato varieties are now widely planted in hanging

27

Growing bags are becoming more popular as the trend for townhouse and condominium living expands.

baskets. Popular for barrel and pyramid planters for many years, strawberries are also being planted in hanging baskets. Pendulous branches, clothed in dark green foliage, provide an attractive background for clusters of bright red berries.

Compact vining habit also makes Patio Pik cucumber an attractive hanging basket plant. Bright yellow flowers precede the production of pickling size cucumbers throughout the growing season.

Tub size varieties have been around for the past several years. One of the best known is Patio Tomato, producing sizable crops of 4 oz. fruit. Its short vine can be trained to a stake.

Eggplant varieties, with short vines and small, but tasty fruit, are also available. Slim Jim, an F-1 Hybrid, has been developed especially for container culture. Fruit is 6-in. long and is produced in clusters.

Because of its compact growth habit and relatively small fruit, Yellow Baby Watermelon can also be grown successfully in a patio tub. Fruit are 10 pounds and have sweet yellow flesh.

These novelty vegetables and fruits are fun because of their uniqueness. However, a wide variety of other crops can be grown in containers.

Green beans are successful in nearly any fairly shallow, well-drained container. The same type of container will suffice for icicle onions and radishes. Shallower still, trays can be used for some types of herbs.

If you have a small garden plot, but do not feel your labor worthwhile for the small yield expected, remember that you can nearly double your production by growing crops vertically. Vertical gardening allows you to plant rows closer together, greatly increasing the number of plants per square foot. Squash, runner beans, tomatoes, cucumbers and other vegetables with trailing stems can be staked, trained to a trellis or one of the new frame and net commercial vegetable growing supports.

Remember, that this kind of cropping practice takes more nutrients out of the soil than regular gardening and that a stepped up program utilizing organic and inorganic fertilizers must be employed.

Increased fertilization is also necessary in containers: (1) Because the volume of soil in containers is limited, available plant nutrients are quickly used by the plant. (2) Because increased waterings are necessary in container culture, plant foods are washed out of the root zone more quickly.

Also necessary for plant health in containers is to use a commercial potting soil rather than soil from the garden. Potting soil has the right consistency for container gardening. It also is sterilized, so the incidence of soil borne insects and disease is kept to a minimum.

Coarse pieces of clay pot or stones should be placed over drain holes in the bottom of the container, followed by a layer of gravel. Add potting soil to within an inch of the container lip.

Cauliflowers

Cauliflower is not the easiest crop because the plants need a long growing season that should be cool when the plants start to form heads – in the fall in most regions.

Soil
The better the soil, the better the cauliflower. Dig in as much organic matter as possible, which can be home-made compost, leafmold, peat moss, rotted manure and any other humus-building materials available locally. Before planting, rake in the standard dose of a complete fertilizer, such as 5–10–5, using 3oz per sq yd (100g per sq m).

When to sow
For most Northern gardens, where the harvest will be in the fall, sow seeds indoors in early to mid-spring and plant resulting seedlings outdoors about 6 weeks later. In the South and other mild-winter regions, seeds should be sown from late summer to late fall.

How to sow and plant
Sow a small quantity of seed very thinly in a flat or special seed tray, covering the seeds lightly and keeping moist until germination. A minimum temperature of 50°F (10°C) is required. Transplant the seedlings, as soon as true leaves appear, into peat pots and grow on a sunny windowsill or about 6in (15cm) from fluorescent tubes. Set plants outdoors 5 to 6 weeks later, either first into a cold frame for gradual hardening off or set in the open ground under Hotkaps for a few weeks. The seedlings will endure some frost once properly hardened off. Space seedlings in the garden from 18 in (45 cm) to 24 in (60 cm) apart. The plants should be watered as necessary and a second feeding of fertilizer given when the heads start to form. White varieties of cauliflower require blanching: tie the leaves over the head when it is about the size of a tennis ball.

Time to germination
7–10 days.

Season of use
According to climate – from summer through autumn, winter and spring. Freezer life: 6 months.

Good varieties
In the South: February, November–December and Mayflower. Elsewhere Show King Hybrid, Snowball types. Purple Head requires no blanching. Its purple heads turn green when cooked.

Protect young cauliflower seedlings with an adjustable garden frame.

Cauliflowers of the Snowball type are grown throughout North America.

Cabbages for summer and fall

The cabbage addict can have this vegetable all the year round. Here we deal with those sown from late winter to spring, and cut from early summer to fall.

Soil
Dig well and incorporate some organic manure. Dried poultry manure, which has a fairly high nitrogen content, is a good choice. Before planting, rake in 3 oz per sq yd (100 g per sq m) of general fertilizer. If at any time the plants seem to be 'standing still', top dress with 1 oz per sq yd (33 g per sq m) of sulphate of ammonia, hoed and, if necessary, watered in.

When to sow and plant
Varieties listed as summer-maturing should be sown as early in spring as possible, preferably in February indoors. Autumn varieties are sown in April or May. Plant from early April to June. Plants are usually quite easy to buy during that period.

How to sow and plant
The early summer cabbages are sown in seed trays indoors if no greenhouse is available. Prick out, harden off, and plant out in April. Or sow in shallow drills, 6 in (15 cm) apart, outdoors in mid-spring and thin out early. The larger and later summer varieties and the autumn types are sown in a prepared seed-bed a few weeks later in drills ½–¾ in (2 cm) deep and 2 in (2 cm) apart and thinned to at least 1 in (2·5 cm). Many varieties are obtainable as pelleted seed and this is one way of ensuring well-spaced seedlings. Plant out when about 3 in (7·5 cm) tall. Planting distances are: early small-headed varieties, 18 in (45 cm) either way; larger and later ones, 18 in (45 cm) in the rows and 24 in (60 cm) between rows.

Time to germination
7–14 days. Cabbage seed, like that of other brassicas, remains viable for several years and a surplus should not therefore be thrown away.

Season of use
June to August for the earlies, August to November for later varieties.

Good varieties
Earliana (60 days), Early Jersey Wakefield (63 days), Copenhagen Market (72 days), Stonehead Hybrid (70 days), Emerald Acre (61 days), Hybrid Emerald Cross (63 days). The last is reputed to stand a long time without splitting.

Above: Small cabbages will form on the stump of a cut spring-maturing cabbage.

Left: Fine summer cabbages. They need good soil and adequate watering.

Below: A fine specimen of a spring-maturing cabbage.

Broccoli

Broccoli matures in most home gardens in late summer and fall. Even the smallest plot has space for a few plants of this high-quality crop.

Soil
Any reasonably good soil will do, but the best quality broccoli is produced on soil treated as advised for summer cauliflowers. If planted in succession to early peas or lettuce, a dressing of 3 oz per sq yd (100 g per sq m) of complete fertilizer should be hoed in before planting.

When to sow and plant
Indoors in early spring, following same method as for cauliflower. Or sow in a seed-bed in April or early May and plant out in June. Or sow direct where it is to grow in June.

How to sow and plant
Sow in the seed-bed as advised for other brassicas, planting out 18 in (45 cm) between plants and between rows. Or sow where the plants are to grow in early June in a drill ½–¾ in (2 cm) deep in groups of seeds 18 in (45 cm) apart. Thin by stages to one plant per group. Water the drill thoroughly before sowing in dry weather.

Brassica seedlings frequently need protection from birds, and where this is the case, protection by nylon net is more easily given when the plants are grouped closely in a seed-bed than when strung out sparsely in a long row. Where bird damage is likely, the seed-bed/transplanting method may be preferable to direct sowing for seedlings liable to attack soon after sowing.

Time to germination
7–14 days, according to time of year.

Season of use
August to November and possibly later in a mild autumn. Broccoli freezes well, the sprigs having a freezer life of six months.

Good varieties
Green Comet, a very early single-headed type with few side shoots. Premium Crop, similar to Green Comet but matures later. De Cicco, producing a central head followed by a large crop of side-shoots.

The tender autumn-maturing broccoli is becoming increasingly popular. The picture shows the central head, which is harvested first, and the smaller sprouts which follow it.

Special note
The plant normally forms a central cluster of buds like a rough green cauliflower. Earlier types produce many lateral shoots when the central head is cut, and such varieties still give the longest-lasting crop. Recent hybrids, however, have been bred to form a larger head at the expense of the side-shoots, and these varieties do not furnish pickings over a long period.

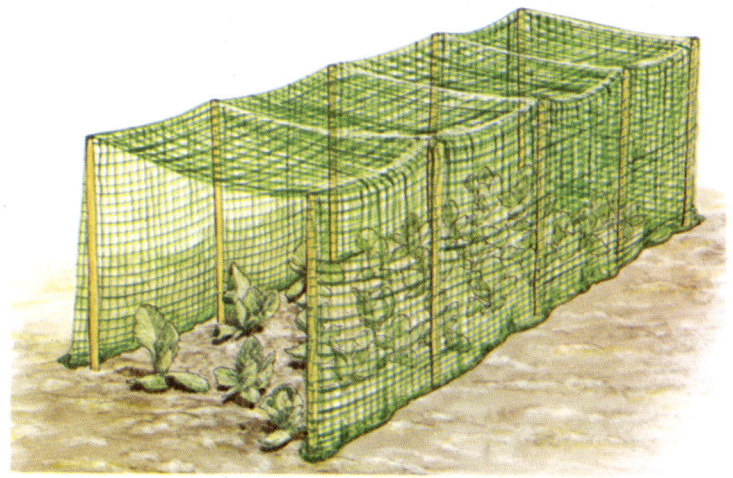

Protect young seedlings by grouping them closely in a seed-bed and covering with nylon net.

Kale

Because of its extreme hardiness kale is regarded as a 'coarse' vegetable. In fact, if the more tender inner leaves are harvested, it is one of the best of winter greens.

Soil
Dig deeply and leave the soil in a condition to ensure good drainage. This should have been done for the crop preceding kale, which is usually sown or planted after snap beans or peas. A light dressing of complete fertilizer, raked in when clearing and lightly cultivating the ground, is advisable to give the kale a good start, but the crop needs no other feeding.

When to sow and plant
Seeds may be sown in the seed-bed in April and planted out in June, or sown where they are to grow in June or early July.

How to sow and plant
In the seed-bed, sow thinly in shallow drills 6 in (15 cm) apart, thinning to give plenty of space to the seedlings. Plant out 18 in (45 cm) apart with rows 24 in (60 cm) apart. When direct sowing, take out a drill ½–¾ in (2 cm) deep, flood it if the weather is at all dry, and drop groups of seeds at 18 in (45 cm) intervals, thinning the seedlings by stages to one at each station. Gaps may be filled by transplanting. There must be no lack of moisture during or after germination; if the July sowing fails it may be too late to try again.

Time to germination
5–10 days. Very rapid in summer – watch for bird attacks on emerging seedlings.

Season of use
Fall, winter and spring.

Good varieties
Green Curled Scotch (55 days), Dwarf Blue Curled Vates (60 days), Dwarf Siberian (65 days).

Special note
Young leaves can be eaten in salads, either alone or mixed with lettuce and other ingredients.

Dwarf curled kale. Like all kales, this will do well in colder areas where winter cabbage and broccoli are not very successful.

Cabbages for winter and spring

From the gardener's point of view the main difference between these cabbages and the sorts grown for summer and autumn consumption is in the matter of hardiness. A wrong choice of variety can be disastrous.

Savoy cabbage. Very hardy and succeeds on poor soil.

Soil
All cabbages are heavy feeders. Follow the recommendations given for summer and fall. On sandy soils dig in some manure or compost and apply a light dressing of complete fertilizer. On stronger land, especially when the cabbages follow a well-treated previous crop, additional manuring is probably unnecessary.

When to sow and plant
Sow winter varieties in May and transplant in June and July. Sow spring varieties at the end of July to mid-August in mild climates and the South. Transplant between mid-September and mid-October.

How to sow and plant
Sow in a prepared seed-bed as advised for late summer and autumn varieties, moving to permanent quarters when about 3 in (7·5 cm) tall. Winter varieties are spaced at 18 in (45 cm) in the row and 24 in (60 cm) between rows. Spring cabbages are spaced at 9 in (23 cm) in the row and 18 in (45 cm) between rows. The close spacing allows every other cabbage to be pulled for 'spring greens' as soon as a fair amount of leaf has developed, leaving the remainder to reach full size and heart up.

Time to germination
7–10 days.

Season of use
Fall to spring. Solid hearts may be frozen, keeping for six months.

Good varieties
Savoy types: Chieftain Savoy, Savoy King. Winter types: Danish Roundhead, Penn State Ballhead, Premium Flat Dutch, Autumn Marvel.

Special note
In addition to the main cabbage crops listed here, some others are worth growing. There is the red pickling cabbage such as Ruby Ball, useful for purposes other than pickling.

January King, probably the best all-round mid-winter cabbage.

13 Peas and beans

Broad or Fava beans

An easy vegetable to grow, not a universal favorite but rich in proteins and giving back more to the soil than it takes out.

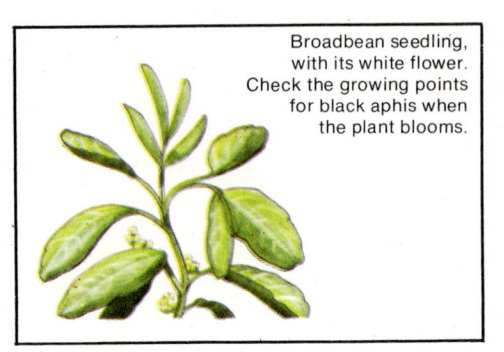

Broadbean seedling, with its white flower. Check the growing points for black aphis when the plant blooms.

Below: A prolific crop of Longpod broad beans. Plants as loaded as this must sometimes be supported by running a length of string along both sides of the row.

Soil
Preferably a cool, moist, rather heavy one, deeply dug well before sowing. On light sands dig in some well-rotted manure or garden compost. Fertilizer is unnecessary.

When to sow
Spring sowings should be made as soon as the soil is dry enough to be raked down to a reasonable condition. The sowing must get established in the cool, damp conditions of early spring. Even quite sharp frosts will not harm the young plants. This is a good crop for many Northern regions because it utilizes garden space in early spring to early summer, and can be succeeded by other crops. Best grown in New England, southern Canada, and similar climates. Grow in winter along the Gulf Coast.

How to sow
In drills at least 6 in (15 cm) wide, 2 to 3 in (5 to 7·5 cm) deep and 24 in (60 cm) apart. Sow two rows in the drill, both the rows and the seeds in each row being 6 in (15 cm) apart in staggered formation. Make the soil firm after covering the drill.

Time to germination
14–21 days.

Season of use
Spring to early summer. Freezer life: 1 year.

Good varieties
Not much choice. Long Pod is usually offered.

Special note
The broad bean has one serious insect pest, the black aphis. It starts in the growing point when the plant is in bloom and may spread down over the pods. Pick out all growing points when a fair number of pods have set. This checks the aphis and speeds up the growth of pods. Or spray with malathion.

Snap and lima beans

Snap beans, formerly called string beans, are available in both bush and pole, or climbing, varieties. Their pods are nutritious and freeze well. Old or mature pods can be shelled and the beans can be cooked fresh or they can be dried.

The lima bean pod must be shelled. It too has both bush and pole varieties, and requires a longer growing season.

The picture below shows just how prolific dwarf beans can be.

Soil
Average garden soil is satisfactory. Apply a complete fertilizer along the rows after the pods form to prolong harvesting.

When to sow
Sow both beans after the soil and temperatures have warmed. Seeds will rot in cold, wet soils. These beans are heat lovers.

How to sow
In drills 2 in (5 cm) deep. The seeds should be 4 in (10 cm) apart and may be sown as a single row in a narrow drill with rows 18 in (45 cm) apart; or as a double row in a wide drill as described for broad beans, the double rows being 24 in (60 cm) apart. Pole beans require support. Set poles 18–24 in (45–60 cm) apart in a row or circle teepee fashion, tying the tops together. Allow 1 seed per pole. Sow extra seeds at one end of the row for filling up any gaps later.

Time to germination
14 days. If no emergence in 21 days, dig up some seeds to discover if seed has rotted owing to low soil temperature.

Season of use
July to September or longer in mild winter climates. Freezer life: 1 year.

Good varieties
Snap bush beans: Improved Tendergreen (56 days), Greensleeves (56 days), Royalty (51 days) has purple pods that turn green when cooked, Goldcrop Wax (54 days), Roma (53 days) has flat pods. Pole snap beans: Kentucky Wonder (65 days), Romano Italian Pole (60 days), Blue Lake (60 days). Bush lima beans: Henderson Bush (65 days), Kingston (70 days). Pole lima beans: King of the Garden (88 days), Prizetaker (90 days).

Special note
Germination is sometimes erratic owing to sowing too early or too deep. Sowing at 2 in (5 cm) is the maximum depth, though the later sowings in light soils dry out rapidly at this depth and should be kept watered until the beans are well up.

Peas

Garden peas, so called to distinguish them from the very different asparagus and sugar peas, are a most important summer crop, both for immediate consumption and for freezing as well.

Soil
A medium or heavy moisture-holding soil is preferred, but peas do quite well on lighter land if some manure or compost is dug in during the winter. They do not like acid conditions, and if there is any doubt on this score lime should be applied after digging. Fertilizer is not necessary where manure or compost has been used.

Right: Peas supported by strings along both sides of the row. The crop may be damaged if allowed to lie flat on the ground in a wet season.

Below: Early peas Kelvedon Wonder, one of the best for the earliest sowing of the year, indoors or in the open.

When to sow
Early varieties, February to March indoors, March and April in the open and again in June for the latest crop. Maincrops, March to May.

How to sow
In drills 6 in (15 cm) wide, 2 to 3 in (5 to 7·5 cm) deep and 24 in (60 cm) apart. Early sowings are made in the shallower drills, late ones in the deeper. The seeds need not be spaced individually but should be scattered evenly and generously in the drill so that a good plant population is obtained. Make sure that the soil of the drill is moist for the late sowings, if necessary by a thorough watering before sowing.

Time to germination
10–21 days. Be prepared to protect from birds, which often discover the emerging seedlings before they are visible to the human eye.

Season of use
June to September from successional sowings. Year-round when frozen.

Good varieties
Indoors, Histon Mini, Feltham First, Hurst Beagle. Early outdoor sowings, Pioneer, Kelvedon Wonder. Maincrops, Early Onward, Onward, Hurst Green Shaft. Latest sowing, one of the first three earlies given above.

Special note
Only dwarf varieties are recommended but even these need some support. Short, twiggy peasticks are excellent but are now rarely obtainable. A neat alternative is to drive in wooden stakes or canes at intervals of 6–7 ft (2 m) along both sides of the row and close to it, running two or three strands of stout garden twine tightly from stake to stake and enclosing the row in a string fence to prevent it flopping sideways.

Asparagus peas and sugar peas

The asparagus pea is not a true pea but a relative of the climbing cowpea. It is half-hardy and must not be exposed to frost. It does not grow in a thickly sown row but as separate bushy plants with attractive pinkish flowers. The sugar pea or mangetout is grown like the garden pea, but the edible parts are the pod and the seeds. The same applies to the asparagus pea.

Season of use
July to September.
Freezer life: 1 year.

Good varieties
Dwarf Gray Sugar (65 days) and Sweetpods (68 days). There are no named varieties of asparagus pea.

Special note
Edible podded peas must be harvested at the correct stage or they are simply uneatable. Sugar peas must be picked when well grown and fleshy but before the seeds have developed. Asparagus peas are gathered when the pods are about 1 in (2·5 cm).

Below: Sugar peas picked at the right stage. The pods must not be left until visibly swollen.

Soils
No special preparation is needed for soils in good average condition, but any lime deficiency should be remedied by a dressing of garden lime after winter digging.

When to sow
Sugar peas are sown from late March to May. Asparagus peas may be started in peat pots indoors in early spring and planted out in May when frost is no longer expected, or sown in the open in early May.

How to sow
Sugar peas are sown in drills 2 in (5 cm) deep exactly as advised for garden peas. Asparagus peas may be sown in seed compost in small peat pots, three seeds to a pot and 1 in (2·5 cm) deep, and started in the frame or on the windowsill. Reduce the seedlings to one per pot and plant out in late May. Alternatively, they may be sown in small groups in a narrow drill and reduced to one seedling at each station by thinning in stages. Whether planted out or direct-sown the plants should stand finally at 18 in (45 cm) apart.

Time to germination
10–21 days. Asparagus peas are rather erratic in germination outdoors though more consistent in pots.

Runner beans

Most Americans know this bean as an ornamental vine grown for its attractive flowers, responsible for its name, scarlet runner. In England and on the Continent the vines are more prized for their edible pods and seeds, which can be used like lima beans. As a vegetable, the vines require a long growing season, about 120 days.

Soil
Some organic materials should be dug in during spring, and supplemented with 3 oz per sq yd (100 g per sq m) of a general fertilizer, raked in 14 days before sowing. Biweekly feeds of liquid fertilizer from the time the plants start to bloom, watering and overhead spraying in hot weather, and mulch, are as important as the initial state of the soil. Just as important too is a situation sheltered from strong winds.

When to sow
In the North sow seeds indoors in peat pots in early spring. In mild climates sow seeds outdoors when the soil has warmed sufficiently.

How to sow
In narrow drills 2 in (5 cm) deep, with the seeds 4 in (10 cm) apart. For growing up poles, sow two rows 12 in (30 cm) apart, placing a row of poles along the outside of both rows of beans and tying the poles together at the top to form a stable inverted V-shaped structure. Sow a few extra beans to provide transplants for gaps.

Time for germination
14 days.

Season of use
Summer to fall if all the pods are picked when young.

Good varieties
American catalogs list only one variety, Scarlet Runner.

Special note
Runner beans, like all leguminous plants, should not be pulled after cropping. Tops should be cleared away and the roots left in the ground to release their accumulated nitrogen.

Above: how to stake a continuous row.
Left: "wigwam" staking for small groups. Use bamboo canes, which last for many years.

Heavy-cropping runner beans like this are produced by good soil, watering and mulching.

14 Permanent crops

Asparagus

This semi-luxury crop is not difficult to grow and an established bed remains in production for up to twenty years. It is now usually grown on the flat rather than on raised beds.

Soil
Asparagus may be grown in any type of soil, though the crop is easier on light land. Eliminate all perennial weeds by thorough cultivation, as it is impossible to do so after planting without damaging the asparagus roots. Dig deeply and if necessary break up the subsoil to ensure good drainage. Work in some manure or compost and about a month before planting fork the soil over and break up any clods.

When to plant
Mid-March to mid-April.

How to plant
Order one-year-old plants early in the season from a good nurseryman. Do not unpack the roots until you are ready to start planting and never leave them exposed, even for an hour, to sun and wind. Take out a trench 12 in (30 cm) wide and 8 in (20 cm) deep. Plant the roots 18 in (45 cm) apart in the trench, sitting each clump on a small heap of soil so that the fleshy roots have a downward slant. Cover carefully with fine soil and fill the trench in.

Cut no shoots the first year but encourage growth by watering freely and also by giving an occasional feed of liquid manure.

Season of use
April to June. Spears may be cut for a short period in the second season after planting and a full crop cut the following year. All cutting should cease in early summer to allow strong growth of the 'tops' and strengthening of the plant for next year's crop. Freshly cut asparagus will freeze well. Freezer life: 9 months.

Good varieties
Martha Washington. The strain is more important than the variety. Order from a specialist nurseryman.

Special note
When hoeing near a row draw the soil towards it, creating a low ridge. Cover with a layer of compost or rotted manure or compost in winter, top dress with 3 oz per sq yd (100 g per sq m) of complete fertilizer in February or March and after harvesting.

During the season all shoots should be cut – thin and deformed ones as well as fine spears like these.

Newly planted asparagus crown, arranged on a little mound of soil at the bottom of the trench so the roots spread downwards.

39

Globe artichokes

The globe artichoke requires a lot of space to produce its edible flower buds and so is not an economical crop for the small garden. It is, however, an impressive plant, and individual specimens may be dotted about and look quite decorative if a row is out of the question.

Left: Cut off suckers as close as possible to where they start growing.

Soil
It must be well-drained and the site open and free from tree-drip. Plants that die in the winter are usually killed by a combination of cold and wet. Work in manure, compost and any available bonfire ashes during digging. Before planting rake in a dressing of general fertilizer.

When to plant
Plant in April, ordering the plants in advance from the nursery. They may be grown from seed but this is rather a long business.

How to plant
Globe artichokes are often planted much too closely. Allow 3 to 4 ft (1 to 2 m) between plants in the row and between rows. Plant very firmly and water after planting in dry weather.

Season of use
Late summer. In the first season there will not be many heads worth using and the plants will be getting established and making growth. Normally, the large terminal buds form first and should be picked before the scales on them begin to turn purple. They are followed by smaller buds on lateral shoots. The artichokes deteriorate rapidly when cut and should be used or frozen as soon as possible after harvesting. Freezer life: 1 year.

Good varieties
Not much choice, but Green Globe is a common variety.

Special note
The plants remain profitable for three years and must then be replaced. Propagate by taking suckers or offsets from the base of adult plants and establishing a new row in April of the third year. Protect plants in winter by covering them with straw.

Below: Harvest heads of artichoke before the scales begin to turn purple.

15 Salad crops

Celery

Blanching or trenching celery is grown in a trench and earthed up to blanch the stems and render them edible. Self-blanching types are grown on the flat and not earthed up. They are mild in flavor and of good quality, but cannot be left in the ground after the beginning of winter frosts.

Above: Plant celery in the bottom of a trench leaving the excavated soil on either side for earthing up.

Below: Blanched or trenching celery. Self-blanching are usually shorter and sometimes green.

Soil
Dig in plenty of moisture-holding organic matter, compost, manure or peat before planting. For blanching varieties the trench should be prepared at this time and manure dug into the bottom of it. Make it 18 in (45 cm) wide and 12 in (30 cm) deep and leave the excavated soil in a ridge beside it for earthing up.

When to sow and plant
Sow seed indoors about 10 weeks before night temperatures reach 50–60°F (10–16°C). Plants are available from the nurseryman in May and June.

How to sow and plant
It is much simpler to buy plants than to raise them, especially as only a limited number are required. If, however, it proves difficult to order the variety you want, sow seed *very* thinly in a tray or flat. Enclose the flat in a plastic bag until the seedlings appear. Prick out the seedlings 2 in (5 cm) apart as soon as you can handle them, using more plastic to cover them for a few weeks. Plant out when 3 in (7·5 cm) tall, one row down the center of the trench, 9 in (22·5 cm) apart, and the self-blanching varieties should be the same distance, both in and between the rows.

Season of use
Late summer to late fall, and longer in mild climates. Celery can only be frozen if it has been cooked and used as a vegetable. Freezer life: 1 year.

Good varieties
Summer Pascal, Golden Self-blanching.

Special note
The growing plants need lots of water. Earth up trench varieties in mid-August, tying the stems of each plant loosely together. Pack soil carefully round to half its height. Repeat monthly until the trench is a ridge with only tips showing.

Chicory

This valuable winter salad is generally neglected by the amateur gardener although it is an interesting crop to grow. The home-grown product will not equal the solid white heads of imported chicory in appearance but it will be fresh and crisp.

Chicory is a biennial plant, making growth and a substantial root one year, dying down and shooting up to flower the following year. The part eaten is the beginning of the second year's growth, grown in darkness so that is blanched and cut before the leaves unfold.

Soil
Any good garden soil, well dug to allow good root development and easy lifting. Wild chicory is a chalkland plant and a dressing of lime should be given if the soil is at all acid.

When to sow
May or June. The latter month is best as a number of plants from early sowings usually bolt and send up premature flower stems.

How to sow
In shallow drills 12 in (30 cm) apart. Sow thinly and thin the seedlings to a final distance of 9 in (23 cm). This distance is a minimum for the development of good plants, as overcrowding and shortage of moisture are two more causes of bolting. So thin rigorously and also water freely in dry weather.

Time to germination
10–14 days. The seedlings are too bitter to suffer much from birds or from insect pests.

Season of use
December to March.

Good varieties
Witloof

Special note
The chicory roots should be lifted very carefully when the tops die down in autumn, placed in a shallow trench and covered with soil or peat so that they may be withdrawn a few at a time for blanching. Remove dead leaves but take care not to damage the crown.

To blanch, place a number of roots close together in a deep pot or plastic bucket, fill with soil-less compost or a mixture of soil, sand and peat to the level of the crowns, and place in a *completely dark* cupboard or cellar. Keep the compost uniformly moist and so long as the temperature is over 50°F (10°C) the heads will develop.

Fine heads of Witloof chicory, showing the type of root necessary to produce them.

Cucumbers

Here we are concerned with cucumbers that can be grown outdoors with or without some protection.

Bottom: One of the improved types of outdoor cucumber, which is of excellent quality.

Below: Prepare continuous mounds of soil and compost on which to plant out rows of cucumber.

Soil
Cucumbers require sun and good drainage, and, at the same time, plenty of moisture, best supplied by incorporating generous amounts of organic matter – rotted manures, compost, peat moss, leafmold – in their growing areas. If there is any doubt as to whether the soil is well-drained, form the planting site into a low mound before sowing seeds or setting out plants. A mulch helps.

When to sow and plant
Cucumbers grow quickly from seeds sown in the open ground after frost danger is passed. However, for an early harvest seeds can be sown indoors about 4 weeks before outdoor sowing is safe. Grow under fluorescent lights or on a sunny windowsill.

How to sow and plant
Sow two or three seeds to a small pot, reducing to one seedling if more than one germinates. Sow in seed compost and preferably in peat pots so that there is no root disturbance in planting out. If the plants are to trail on the ground the planting areas should be 3 ft (90 cm) apart, but if they are to be trained up a trellis or other support only 18 in (45 cm) apart. Water in when planting and do everything possible to shelter plants from cold winds.

Time to germination
Cucumber seeds germinate quickly, but only if a temperature of about 64°F (18°C) can be maintained. A propagator is useful. Sow ½ in (2 cm) deep, placing the seeds on edge.

Season of use
July to October.

Good varieties
Burpee's Hybrid, Victory Hybrid, China, Burpless.

Special note
When grown as ground trailers the plants should be stopped at six leaves to encourage the growth of laterals. In climbers, the main stem is tied to the supports and pinched off when it reaches the top. Laterals are also tied. Only they are allowed to fruit.

Endive

Endive is a popular salad ingredient in fall and winter. Since it is more tender and flavorful after blanching, a process that requires time and effort, it may not be a crop that appeals to every home gardener.

Curled endive before blanching. The delicate leaves are liable to decay under damp conditions.

Soil
Plant in a soil rich in organic matter – rotted manure, compost, peat moss – and add a complete fertilizer before sowing as recommended for lettuce.

When to sow
July is the best month if only one sowing is to be made.

How to sow
In narrow drills ½–¾ in (2 cm) deep. As this sowing takes place at the hottest time of the year the drill should be thoroughly soaked beforehand and kept damp until germination. The seedlings will also need watering in dry weather. If more than one row is grown they should be 12 in (30 cm) apart, and that should also be the final spacing of the plants after thinning. The plants must not be allowed to overlap or the dense, curly foliage will start to rot. Seed may be sown thinly as there are usually few losses of seedlings from birds or other causes.

Time to germination
10–14 days.

Season of use
Fall and winter.

Good varieties
Green Curled, Batavian Broad Leaved, Florida Deep Heart, Witloof Chicory.

Special note
The blanching of endive is essential; the leaves are bitter and inedible until they have lost their green color. About three months after sowing, start tying the outside leaves over the hearts. Or cover the plants with a long board or buckets, flower pots with the drainage holes covered, or anything to keep them warm and dry and completely in the dark. Plants can be packed in a cold frame and blanched as needed through much of the winter.

Lettuce

One of the most important ingredients of the salad bowl, lettuce is easy to grow but less easy to grow well. The secrets are a fairly good soil, adequate moisture in summer, and frequent small sowings.

Soil
Choose a sunny site (some shade in summer is acceptable) and a soil that is rich in organic matter. Add peat moss, rotted manure and compost before sowing or planting.

When to sow
Spring is the big season for lettuce in most of the North. Sow seeds outdoors as soon as soil can be worked, usually in late March-April. Sowing indoors 3–4 weeks before then or in a cold frame or heated frame speeds the harvest. Make small sowings every 10 days or so until early summer. Start sowings outdoors again in late summer for fall use. In mild climates, lettuce grows best in cool weather – fall, winter, spring.

How to sow
In short drills or broadcast over seed-bed ½–¾ in (2 cm) deep. Start thinning when first true leaves appear, or transplant 5–10 in (12·5–25·5 cm) apart, according to variety.

Season of use
Spring, summer, fall and through winter in mild climates.

Time to germination
10–14 days.

Good varieties
A wealth of variety is available – consult seed catalogs. Choose from among butterhead or cabbage, looseleaf, or head types. Bibb, Buttercrunch, Tom Thumb are all butterhead types that are small and mature in about 75 days. A larger butterhead is Dark Green Boston (80 days). Among looseleaf varieties are Ruby, Oak Leaf and Salad Bowl (see below), all fairly heat tolerant. Among head lettuce varieties are Great Lakes and cos or romaine types.

Special note
A new development has been the advent of the leaf lettuce, a non-hearting type from which leaves are taken as required without cutting the whole plant. A good variety is Salad Bowl.

Above: Modern varieties of cos lettuce are self-folding and do not need to be tied.

Below: The other main type is the cabbage group of lettuce, and there are many varieties from which to choose.

Radishes and salad onions

These two salad crops are useful short-term fillers of the odd space as well as being essential to the complete salad list. They sometimes disappoint for want of a little care.

Radishes and spring or salad onions. Grow them as catch crops on any small area available.

Soil
Any soil in reasonably good health, as one manured for a previous crop, will do for these crops. The worst soils, especially for radishes, are very poor, dry ones. A little garden compost forked in before the ground is leveled for sowing is a help, but do not use large quantities of organic manures or fertilizers.

When to sow
Radishes, as early as the ground can be worked in the spring, and thereafter every 10 days or so up to early summer. Sow again in late summer for fall crops. Radishes do not withstand heat. Onions, March to July, remembering that if you are growing onions for storage there should be plenty of thinnings for a time in May or June. A final sowing of onions for spring use may be made in September, wintering unprotected in mild districts.

How to sow
Both crops are sown in drills ½–¾ in (2 cm) deep and 6 in (15 cm) apart. Sow thinly and thin the radishes further if the seedlings are at all crowded. The commonest cause of failure with radishes is not giving the roots room to develop. Salad onions may be left fairly thick and withdrawn for use as soon as they are large enough.

Time to germination
Radishes, 5–10 days.
Onions, 14–21 days.

Above: Oval radish French Breakfast. An old variety, unbeatable for quality.

Season of use
Spring to autumn.

Good varieties
Radish: Scarlet Globe, Sparkler, Cherry Belle (globe-shaped), French Breakfast, Summer Grass Hybrid, a giant white oriental type that remains crisp and mild. Onions: White Lisbon. The pickling onion, White Portugal, is grown like salad onions, sown in spring, and lifted when the roots are as big as marbles.

Below: unthinned radishes, roots unusable. *(left):* properly thinned or sown very thinly *(right).*

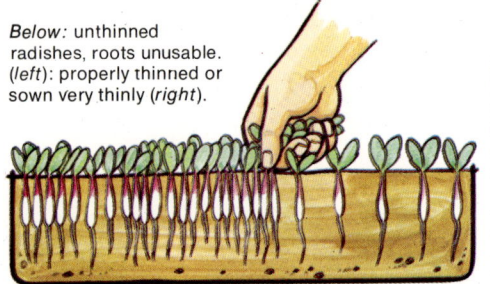

Special note
It is far better to sow salad onions than to rely entirely on the main onion bed for the supply of 'spring' onions. This leads to onions too large for the salad and too crowded, owing to delayed thinning to make good storage bulbs.

Tomatoes

The tomato ranks as the most popular home garden vegetable. Culture can be complicated and laborious, or a few plants from the local garden center can be stuck in the ground and produce a miracle harvest. Study catalog descriptions of varieties suitable for containers on terraces as well as greenhouse and garden growing.

Soil
If possible, select a position on the south side of a wall or fence and dig thoroughly. Rake in 3 oz per sq yd (100 g per sq m) complete fertilizer before planting. When plants are fruiting, feed regularly with a high-potash liquid fertilizer.

When to sow and plant
Buy plants from a local nursery and plant out in late spring. Alternatively sow seed in early April, harden off and plant out under Hotkaps in mid-May.

How to sow and plant
Sow in seed compost in trays in the greenhouse, on a light windowsill or anywhere maintaining a temperature of 60°F (16°C). Prick out seedlings into peat pots of potting compost after the first true leaves appear, grow on to 15 cm (6 in) under fluorescent lights to ensure sturdy growth, and harden off in the frame before planting out. Tall varieties are planted 18 in (45 cm) apart, and each is tied to a stout cane. Bush or dwarf varieties, are planted 24 in (60 cm) apart.

Time to germination
10–14 days in the right temperature. Very early pricking out of the small seedlings is essential.

Season of use
July to November. The last of the crop is ripened indoors. Tomatoes for cooking may be frozen; storage life, 1 year.

Good varieties
Early Girl Hybrid, Big Girl Hybrid VF, Better Boy Hybrid VFN. Small-fruited bush varieties: Small Fry, Pixie, Early Salad.

Special note
Tall varieties are grown as a single stem. Nip out all side-shoots as soon as they show in the leaf axils. Remove the growing point after the third or fourth truss has set. Restrict the number of branches on bush varieties to three or four.

Some top-quality varieties of miniature tomatoes make decorative pot plants.

Good full-size tomato specimens.

Pot-grown tomatoes on a patio. Keep them to a single stem by pinching out side-shoots (see inset) as soon as they appear in the leaf axils. Pinch out growing points of outdoor plants when three trusses of fruit have set.

47

16 Root crops

Beets

Beet succeeds on most soils provided its growth is not checked by cold or drought, which may cause it to bolt instead of forming a proper root or to produce roots that are tough and woody. Do not sow it too early in spring and be prepared to water it on light, dry soils.

Certain varieties of beet are grown for their edible leaves and stems instead of for their roots (see perpetual spinach).

Soil
A complete fertilizer may be raked in well before sowing at the rate of 3 oz per sq yd (100 g per sq m) but on land in good heart after manuring for a previous crop this may not be necessary.

When to sow
Beets are very hardy. Start sowing in early spring (about April 1 in most Northern areas) and make successive sowings, where space permits, up to early summer to maintain a supply of small beets to use fresh (with their tops) as well as older beets for storage.

How to sow
In drills 1 in (2·5 cm) deep and 12 in (30 cm) apart. For midsummer sowings in dry weather, water the drills before sowing and keep watered until seedlings emerge. Beet 'seeds' are usually clusters of seeds, so don't sow too thickly. Protect from birds with netting or black thread if necessary.

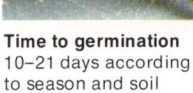

Time to germination
10–21 days according to season and soil temperature.

Season of use
Fresh and stored, late June to late February. Freezer life: good condition for six months.

Good varieties
Golden Beet, good for tops and roots; Lutz Green Leaf, Winter Keeper, for greens and roots for storing; Detroit Dark Red Medium Top, for greens and roots for storing; Cylindra, long roots for slicing.

Special note
Start thinning beet as soon as the first true leaves appear. Thin in stages to 1, 2 and 4 in (2·5, 5, and 10 cm) using sizeable roots from the last stage. At the first thinning, take care to reduce to one seedling the little clumps that often emerge from each seed.

Above: Golden Beet. This new variety does not bleed like the ordinary red types. Its quality is excellent and the leaves may be cooked like spinach.

Left: Globe beet, best for winter storage. Semi-flat early-maturing beet.

Carrots

The carrot is one of the most useful of root vegetables, pulled young and tender from successional sowings in summer, kept in that condition in the freezer, or stored naturally when mature for use throughout the winter.

Soil
Light land produces the finest long carrots, but the stump-rooted and cylindrical varieties do well on heavy land well dug and left rough to weather through the winter. The crop responds to the standard fertilizer dressing of 3 oz per sq yd (100 g per sq m) raked in about two weeks before sowing. No organic manure is needed.

When to sow
From early spring to early summer, choosing a short, quick-growing variety for the latest sowings. Carrots are a useful crop to succeed early peas or spinach.

How to sow
In drills ½–¾ in (2 cm) deep and 9 to 12 in (23 to 30 cm) apart. Monthly sowings will ensure young roots for immediate consumption and freezing over a long period and plenty of full-sized ones for winter storage. Thin by stages to a distance of 3 in (10 cm), using the later thinnings.

Time to germination
14–21 days.

Season of use
Freshly pulled and naturally stored, June to March. Freezer life: 1 year.

Good varieties
On deep soils, Imperator, Gold Pak. On all types of soil, Danvers Half Long, Royal Chantenay. Recommended for freezing, Goldinhart, Nantes.

Special note
The major pest of the carrot is the carrot fly, whose larvae scar and distort the roots. It is controlled more by management than by pesticides. Choose an open and exposed site for the carrot bed as the fly prefers a sheltered habitat. It is attracted to the crop for egg-laying by the smell of the carrots, frequently when they are disturbed during thinning. Thin on a dull day or after sunset, firm and water the seedlings after thinning and, best of all, use pelleted seed sown ½–¾ in (2 cm) apart and reduce thinning to a minimum.

Left: Forked carrots are caused by manuring the ground with manure just before sowing.

Right: The long, cylindrical type of carrot which gives its best performance on deep, well-cultivated soils.

Above: Carrot Chantenay. An intermediate variety, red-cored, early and fine for freezing.

Celeriac

Also known as turnip-rooted celery, this rather unattractive-looking root serves a useful purpose. It is a celery-flavored vegetable and may be used in cooking as a celery substitute, or parboiled and marinated, then served as a salad. It will grow where celery consistently fails, is less trouble to cultivate and may be lifted and stored for winter like other root vegetables.

Soil
Well-manured soil that will hold moisture is essential for succulent roots. If manure is short, dig in plenty of peat on the site of the row and rake in a dressing of general fertilizer before planting out.

When to sow
Start seeds indoors as for celery, or in the open during late spring. Celeriac plants, unlike celery plants, are difficult to buy.

How to sow and plant
Sow thinly in very shallow drills lightly covering the seed with fine soil. Outdoor sowings must be watered in dry weather. The seedlings, like those of celery, are apt to look crowded and fragile, and if you do not want the trouble of pricking out, they may be thinned and left to grow on. In this case you must sow a sufficient length of drill to give the required number of plants when thinned to 2 in (5 cm) apart.

Plant out when the young plants are big enough to handle, 12 in (30 cm) apart in the row with 18 in (45 cm) between rows. Water before lifting and plant so that the roots are covered but the small swelling at the base of the stem rests on the surface. Water carefully after planting to settle the plants.

Time to germination
14–21 days.

Season of use
October to March from the ground and from storage. Not much point in freezing.

Good varieties
Marble Ball, Alabaster, Large Smooth Prague.

Special note
Celeriac is grown on the flat and dries out more than trench celery, although it needs water just as much. Keep it hoed, watered and if possible mulched with peat.

Left and below: Improved types of celeriac. Modern varieties have better-shaped roots than the older forms.

Jerusalem artichokes

The Jerusalem artichoke has no associations with Jerusalem; its name derives from the Italian *girasole*, a sunflower. Its knobby tubers are not universal culinary favorites but it has the advantage of being extremely easy to grow.

Soil
Neither manure nor fertilizer are normally used. The ground should be well dug before planting and forked over again before planting to leave it loose and open.

When to plant
April to May as soon as the soil is workable.

How to plant
In separate holes or a continuous trench 6 in (15 cm) deep, spacing the tubers 12 in (30 cm) apart. Planting tubers may be bought from the seedsman or you can use those bought from the greengrocer for culinary purposes. It is unlikely that more than one row will be required, and as the plants grow a good 6–7 ft (2 m) tall this should be sited where it will least overshadow other crops. In a windy situation it may be necessary to support the tall stems by running a strand of wire or twine, attached to poles or stout canes, along the row.

Time to emergence
Shoots will appear 3–4 weeks after planting.

Jerusalem artichoke tubers bear no resemblance to the globe variety and are cooked quite differently. They take up less planting space than the globes and are a much underrated vegetable – the globe variety being considered a glamorous starter to a luxurious dinner.

Season of use
November to March, the tubers being lifted as required, or stored in a cool place covered with peat if hard frost seems likely to make lifting impossible. The tubers may be frozen but the high-quality storage time is only 3 months, so freezing in the autumn is pointless. The season of use may, however, be prolonged a few months by freezing the tubers in late fall or before growth restarts.

Varieties
There are not any varieties of Jerusalem artichokes which are distinct.

Jerusalem artichokes make a good screen for less attractive items – such as a compost heap.

Special note
This is a difficult plant to eliminate from the garden once you introduce it since every small and broken tuber left in the ground proliferates like a weed. It is better to leave it out of the rotation and confine it to some corner of the plot where it may be grown for several years running.

Onions

This concerns bulb onions for storage. Salad onions are dealt with under that heading.

Soil
Choose an open, sunny site and dig it deeply during the winter. If the onions form part of the root-crop section in the rotation, no manure or compost need be used, but some may be dug in if a special bed is prepared. Onions are one of the few crops that may be grown on the same ground for years if free from disease. Complete fertilizer should be raked in at the rate of 3 oz per sq yd (100 g per sq m) as soon as the soil dries in early spring. Then tread it until quite firm and rake it again to a fine, level tilth.

When to sow or plant
Sow seed as soon as the soil is workable in early spring. Plant sets in April.

How to sow or plant
Seed is sown in drills ½–¾ in (2 cm) deep and 12 in (30 cm) apart. After covering the seed, firm the soil by lightly treading the drills. Thin the seedlings by stages to a final distance of 4 in (10 cm). Use the later thinning for salads but do not be tempted to delay thinning to ensure a supply of 'spring' onions.

Onion sets are small bulbs whose growth was checked the previous season. When planted they start growing again and mature more quickly than seed-grown plants. Take out drills the same distance apart as for seeds, press the sets into the bottom of the drill 4 in (10 cm) apart, and fill in the drill so that only the necks are visible.

Time to germination
14–21 days. Sets begin to root in 14 days.

Season of use
July to March. Chopped or sliced onions may be frozen for two months.

Good varieties
Seed: Early Yellow Globe, Ebenezer, Southport White Globe.
Sets: Ebenezer, Stuttgarter.

Special note
Onion seedlings are small and fragile and should be carefully hand weeded from the time of emergence. If weeds are allowed to get established they can soon smother the young crop. Many mail order nurseries and seed houses, and local garden centers, now offer onion seedlings in the spring. These seedlings will supply mature onions faster than your own seedlings.

Flat onion. The Stuttgarter variety shown here is one of the best to grow from sets.

Globe onion, the most popular type for growing from seed.

Onion sets

Parsnips

The parsnip is a hardy and undemanding vegetable, but perfect long specimens are only grown on deep loams or similar soils. Heavy clay soils must be deeply prepared before sowing parsnip seeds.

Perfect long-rooted parsnips. On heavy clays stump-rooted varieties give better results.

Soil
Dig deeply, breaking up the subsoil if possible, though without bringing any of it to the surface. Try to complete digging early in the winter, leaving the ground rough. If it was manured for the previous crop no fertilizer need be used when preparing to sow. Rake the surface down to a fine tilth.

When to sow
March or April in all districts, when the soil is in workable condition. This crop is not expected to mature until autumn. Always buy fresh seed each year, as old seed will not germinate.

How to sow
Sow in narrow drills ½ in (1·25 cm) deep and 12 in (30 cm) apart. The seed is large enough to be sown quite thinly, but is also very light, and when sowing in a strong wind the hand should be held close to the drill. Thin seedlings by stages to 6 in (15 cm) apart.

Time to germination
14–21 days, but in early spring you should allow 4 weeks before assuming a failure.

Season of use
October to March. Parsnips are left in the ground and lifted as required during the winter. They should not be stored in the freezer.

Good varieties
All-America, broad and somewhat short roots; Marris Model, medium long roots; Hollow Crown, long tapered roots.

Special note
Parsnips do not store well out of the ground and so are better dug only when needed. This becomes difficult during prolonged hard frost, and it pays to keep the row covered with a thick layer of peat to reduce the depth to which the ground is frozen. Lift all unused roots when they begin to grow out in late February or March and store in a cool shed in a box of peat moss.

Potatoes

Early potatoes are a semi-luxury and should be grown if room can be found. Later varieties are only worth growing in the larger garden.

Soil
Potatoes prefer a slightly acid soil rich in humus. Compost or well-rotted manure may be used in the trench when planting but a combination of peat and fertilizer is almost equally good, especially on light sandy soils. The ground should be dug in fall or early spring and forked over again before planting. Potatoes do not need a fine tilth but do best in a loose soil not settled and compacted.

When to plant
Earlies, late March to mid-April. Maincrops, April and early May. Much depends on the frequency of late frosts in your district and nothing is gained by early planting if the growth is cut off. Gain time by getting the 'seed' tubers at least a month before planting and setting them up in trays in a light, frost-proof place to develop sturdy green shoots.

How to plant
Take out a trench 5 in (12·5 cm) deep with the spade. Space the potatoes in it 12 in (30 cm) apart, with the rows 24 in (60 cm) apart for earlies and a little more for maincrops. Cover each tuber with a double handful of peat or compost. Sprinkle complete fertilizer along the trench at the rate of 2 oz per yd (66 g per m) of row. Fill in the trench with the rake or draw-hoe.

Time to emergence
2–4 weeks according to soil temperature. Watch for the shoots and draw soil over them if frost threatens at night.

Season of use
June to the following May. Apart from normal storage of the mature crop, new potatoes may be frozen partially cooked and will keep for up to a year.

Even crop of potato tubers.

Good varieties
Buy certified seed potatoes that are free from disease and are varieties which are recommended for your region.

Special note
Potatoes should be earthed up to encourage tuber formation and prevent tubers greening from exposure to light. Draw the soil up to the stems to form a ridge when the plants are about 8 in (20 cm) tall. If growth seems to have been slow a further light dressing of fertilizer may be scattered near the plants before starting to earth up.

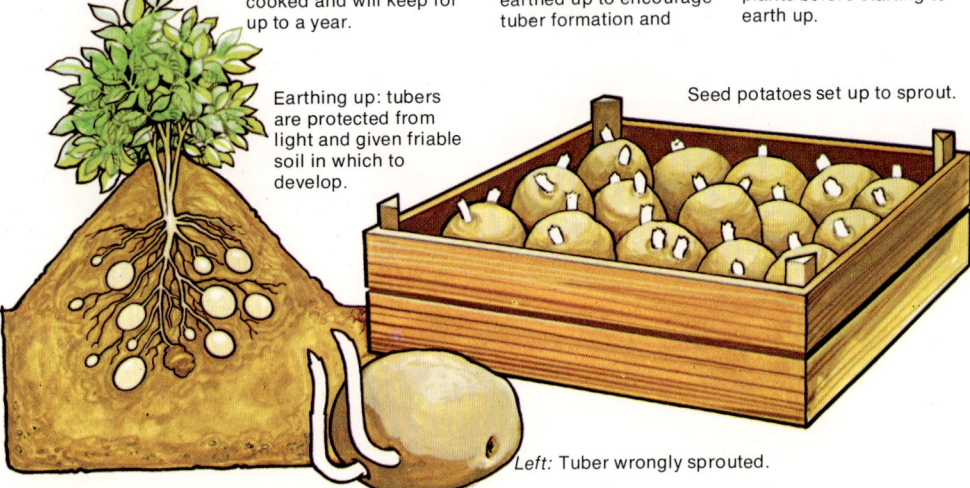

Earthing up: tubers are protected from light and given friable soil in which to develop.

Seed potatoes set up to sprout.

Left: Tuber wrongly sprouted.

Rutabagas

The rutabaga is a useful vegetable and although related to the turnip is different and distinctive in flavor and texture.

Soil
Heavy and loamy soils are better than light ones. As with most crops in the root section of the rotation, the ground should not be manured when dug in the winter, but 3 oz per sq yd (100 g per sq m) of general fertilizer should be raked in before sowing. Rutabagas are an excellent crop to follow early peas, beans or potatoes.

When to sow
Not early. From late spring to early summer so that roots will mature in the fall.

How to sow
In drills ½–¾ in (2 cm) deep and 18 in (45 cm) apart. Sow thinly and start thinning as soon as the seedlings get their first true leaves. Continue thinning in stages to a final distance of 6 in (15 cm). The thinnings are of no culinary use, as rutabagas do not develop their proper flavor until nearing maturity.

Time to germination
7–10 days. Germination of the later sowings is very rapid.

Season of use
October to March from storage. Rutabaga purée keeps for a year in the freezer.

Good varieties
Purple Top Yellow (90 days), Macomber (92 days). The latter variety is particularly recommended both for its keeping qualities and also for its mildness of flavor.

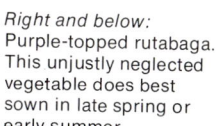

Right and below:
Purple-topped rutabaga. This unjustly neglected vegetable does best sown in late spring or early summer.

Special note
It is a mistake to sow rutabagas too early. The roots are not wanted in the summer and early crops are often badly affected by mildew. Sown in June or early July following the clearance of early peas or potatoes, the crop has plenty of time to mature and is usually healthy. In dry weather, water the drills before sowing and keep the seedlings watered until well-established.

Turnips

Turnips flourish in most gardens, given a consistent supply of moisture. Drought and erratic watering may cause them to bolt and form no root at all or to produce roots strong in flavor and stringy in texture.

Soil
Give turnips a reasonably good garden soil that contains organic matter – compost, rotted manure. Rake in 3 oz per sq yd (100 g per sq m) of complete fertilizer well before the early crop is sown. The late crop should follow peas or spinach and for this a dressing of 1½ oz per sq yd (50 g per sq m) should be hoed in.

When to sow
Turnips are fairly fast to mature and make best growth in cool weather. Sow seeds of Tokyo Cross and Early Purple-Top Milan in early spring in open ground. For fall and winter crops sow seeds about 8 weeks before first expected hard frost.

How to sow
In drills ½–¾ in (2 cm) deep and 15 in (37·5 cm, apart. Turnips should not be crowded at any stage of growth and the leaves need plenty of room to spread. Start thinning when the first rough leaves appear and thin by stages to a final distance apart of 4 in (10 cm), using the small roots from the later thinnings.

Time to germination
5–14 days. June and July sowings, if kept moist, may emerge in 4 days and careful watch must be kept to see that the small seedlings are not being pulled up by birds. Protect with netting or black thread if necessary.

Season of use
From the ground or storage, June onwards and for most of the winter. Freezer life: 1 year.

Good varieties
Early sowing, Tokyo Cross Hybrid, Early Purple-Top Milan. Later sowings, Just Right Hybrid.

Special note
A productive late crop may be obtained from a broadcast sowing. Select a strip about 24 in (60 cm) wide, hoe up weeds and incorporate fertilizer. Rake level, scatter seed thinly over area and cover lightly with fine soil, keeping watered. Thin where crowded.

Purple-top Milan turnip.

Milan turnip, a flat variety. Globe varieties are usually better for earliest sowings.

17 Miscellaneous crops

Leeks

The leek is not only one of the hardiest of the onion family but also the most delicately flavored. Nothing quite replaces it as a winter vegetable.

Soil
Good soil produces large, plump leeks. Dig deeply in spring, working in some manure or compost. Before planting, apply 3 oz per sq yd (100 g per sq m) of a general fertilizer, forking it well into the topsoil.

When to sow and plant
Sow in a seed-bed from early March to mid-April. Plant out from May to July. Give leeks the longest growing season possible.

How to sow and plant
Sow in the seed-bed in shallow drills 6 in (15 cm) apart. Thin the seedlings to 2 in (5 cm) and plant out when about 8 in (20 cm) tall. Well-grown plants are easier to transplant than thin, grassy ones, and for that reason it pays to allow them plenty of space.

Water before lifting, and trim back the longest leaves of the seedlings by about one-quarter of their length before planting. Plant 9 in (23 cm) apart in rows 18 in (45 cm) apart. Make a hole with a dibbler, not quite as deep as the leek plant is long, drop the plant in it, and fill the hole with water. Do not fill it with soil, either then or subsequently. Enough soil is washed down to cover the roots and the stem is left with room for expansion.

Blanch the stems, beginning in late summer when plants are about 6 in (15 cm) high, by pulling soil against the plants up to where the green part of the stem begins.

Time to germination
14–21 days. May be rather slow. Seedlings are practically immune to insect and bird damage.

Season of use
Autumn to spring. Plants are kept in the ground and lifted as required. Leeks may be frozen for use in summer.

Good varieties
Broad London, Conqueror.

Special note
Although leeks survive hard frost, they are almost impossible to lift without damage when the ground is frozen. One solution is to lift the plants and pack them upright in boxes of damp peat moss and soil, and store these in a cool cellar or shed.

Far left: Leek seedlings planted. The holes are filled with water after planting but are not filled up with soil.

Squashes

This is a large and varied group, which also includes zucchini and pumpkins. They all need basically the same treatment and the same humus-rich soil. They are all tender and must not be exposed to frost.

Soil
These vegetables cannot be grown without some organic manure or compost. They do not respond well to inorganic fertilizers. Use the manure or compost to prepare stations for the plants, digging the manure into the soil at each site and raising it into a low mound. Do not leave manure and soil in separate layers. A barrowload of manure is enough for three plants.

When to sow and plant
Indoors: 4 weeks before last frost is expected.
Outdoors: A week before the last frost.

How to sow and plant
Sow in seed compost, preferably in peat pots. Squashes dislike root disturbance in planting out. Sow two or three seeds per pot at a depth of ½–¾ in (2 cm) keeping only the strongest seedling. Do not sow earlier than suggested or the plants will be starved and pot-bound before it is safe to plant them out. Alternatively, sow in the same way on each prepared mound in the first week of June, placing the seeds in little pockets of compost or sifted soil and watering daily if necessary. The prepared sites should be spaced as follows. For bush squashes and zucchini, 2½ ft (75 cm). Most squashes, 3 ft (90 cm). Vining winter squashes and pumpkins, 4 ft (1·2 m).

Time to germination
10–14 days, provided a night temperature of 50°–55°F (10°–13°C) is maintained. In temperatures below this seed is likely to rot.

Right: Zucchini, a productive bush type which may be cut as courgettes or left to grow to full size.

Below: Summer squash.

Below: Squash Vegetable Spaghetti. One of the best of the squashes, with flesh of a distinctive texture.

Season of use
Summer squashes, July to October. Ripened Butternuts, pumpkins and winter squashes, from October to January.

Good varieties
Summer squashes: Vegetable Spaghetti (a vining variety – boil and scoop out center), Baby Crookneck, Seneca Butterbar Hybrid, St Pat Scallop, Greyzini, Aristocrat Hybrid. Fall and winter squashes: Bush Acorn Table King, Butternut, Hubbard.

Melons and watermelons

Melons (cantaloupes and muskmelons) and watermelons do best in mild climates with long growing seasons. Gardeners in the North can be successful if they start the seeds indoors and choose early-maturing varieties.

Soil
Like squashes and cucumbers the melon must be grown on a prepared site. For each plant mix a good pailful of rotted manure or garden compost with the soil taken from a hole about 12 in (30 cm) square. Loosen the soil at the bottom of the hole to promote good drainage and replace the mixture, shaping it into a small mound. The same procedure applies whether the plants are in the open, or in a frame. Distance between planting sites should be 24 in (60 cm).

When to sow and plant
Seed requires a temperature of 60°–70°F (16°–21°C) for germination, and the plants cannot be transplanted to the garden until late May or to the open ground until early June. Therefore, sow seeds indoors about 4 weeks before it is safe to plant outside in peat pots.

How to sow and plant
Raise seedlings as described for cucumbers, remembering that melons are a little more tender. Plant out with the least possible root disturbance, choosing the sunniest, most sheltered site you can find for the unprotected plants. Never allow the plants to suffer from lack of water, using it tepid for young seedlings and watering newly-planted outdoor plants before sunset. Plant under Hotkaps. Mulch with black plastic.

Time to germination
7–10 days in the right temperature.

Season of use
August to October. Freezer life: 1 year.

Good varieties
Muskmelons: Gold Star, Harper Hybrid; Watermelons: Sugar Baby, Yellow Baby.

Special note
The trailing shoots are stopped after the fifth leaf and the laterals they produce are stopped at the third leaf. The fruits are borne on these laterals. Rest the fruit on pieces of tile or polyethylene as they ripen and harvest when they develop the characteristic melon scent and the fruit slips readily from the stem.

Top and left: Cantaloupe melon. Several varieties may be grown in frames, under cloches or even in the open.

Swiss chard

This rather neglected vegetable is another leaf beet, related to perpetual spinach. The edible part is the broad leaf stalk and midrib, pure white in most varieties and pink in the variety Rhubarb. This is a delicious vegetable and should be better known. It is a good summer greens, as it withstands heat well.

Bottom: Ruby Chard, the red form of Swiss chard. A valuable addition to the menu and so decorative that it may be grown in the flower border.

Below: The production of Swiss chard can be prolonged with protection in frosty weather.

Soil
Treat it as for the growing of spinach. The only difference is that Swiss chard is slower in reaching maturity and has time to respond to weekly feeding with liquid fertilizer in addition to regular watering. In well grown plants the edible stems should be 2 in (5 cm) wide.

When to sow
Early to mid-spring. This is a late summer and autumn crop and too tender to carry on into winter.

How to sow
In drills 1 in (2·5 cm) deep and 18 in (45 cm) apart. Thin the seedlings to 4 in (10 cm) apart as soon as they can be handled. A week or so later remove every other plant and leave the remainder at twice this distance. Swiss chard, in both white and pink forms, is quite a decorative plant, and clumps of it may be grown in the shrub or herbaceous borders if kitchen garden space is limited.

Time to germination.
14 days.

Season of use
July to October.

Good varieties
Fordhook Giant,
Rhubarb Chard,
Lucullus,
Perpetual.

Special note
The outer leaves are cut at ground level when large enough and the plant continues to produce more from the center. The leaf is stripped from the midrib and may be cooked like spinach if there is enough of it. Leaf stalks and midribs, which are the main part of the crop, can be cooked separately.

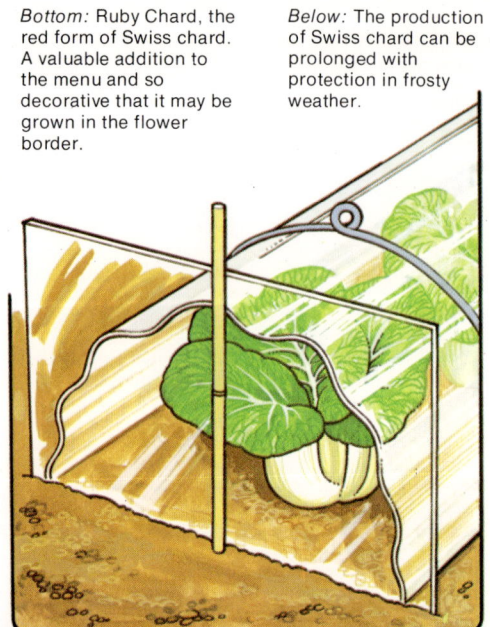

Spinach

Spinach is one of the fastest vegetables to mature. A March sowing is often ready for cutting in late May and sowings at intervals of three weeks will maintain a continuous supply in regions where summers are cool and moist. Elsewhere it is only a spring and fall crop, as it has no heat tolerance.

Soil
Spinach is a leaf crop and must have plenty of moisture and adequate nitrogen to produce abundant foliage. Its worst feature is a tendency to run to seed, and the warmer and drier the soil, the quicker it does so. On heavy clays and very light soils dig in all the humus-forming material you can spare, even if it be only peat. Then, before sowing, rake in 1 oz per sq yd (33 g per sq m) of sulphate of ammonia.

When to sow
Early spring and late summer for fall harvest.

How to sow
The largest crop from a given area is obtained by sowing in a drill about 6 in (15 cm) wide and rather less than 1 in (2·5 cm) deep. Sprinkle the seed thinly and evenly over the bottom of the drill, first soaking it with water if the soil is dry. Fill in and firm the soil. If more than one row is sown the drills should be 12 in (30 cm) apart. Allow the seedlings to grow to about 4 in (10 cm) and then thin for the first time. The thinnings are large enough to use, it being only necessary to snip off the roots. After a few days, the row will have filled up again and more thinnings may be used, the rest of the plants then being spaced widely enough to grow to full size for cutting.

Time to germination
10–14 days.

Season of use
May to October, depending on climate. Young spinach with a minimum of stalk may be frozen. Freezer life: 1 year.

Good varieties
America (50 days), Bloomsdale Long Standing (48 days), Winter Bloomsdale (45 days).

Special note
Spinach is one of the few vegetables to succeed in partial shade – though not in competition with tree roots.

Above: Summer spinach Bloomsdale Long Standing.

Left: Sowing seed for summer spinach.

Perpetual spinach

Also known as spinach beet, the plant is unrelated to summer spinach. It is a leaf beet, a biennial with a strong tap-root that may live for several years, though in practice it should be sown annually. It produces a succession of edible leaves in autumn and spring and, if cloched, throughout the winter.

This vegetable is virtually unknown and uncultivated in the USA, but there's no reason why it can't be grown. Order seeds from British firms.

Soil
Any soil in reasonably good heart is quite suitable if it is well cultivated. The crop is a good follow-up to early potatoes, which leave the soil in the right condition so that it only needs to be raked level before sowing. A light dressing of general fertilizer raked in at that stage helps to get the seedlings away quickly, but more important is to make sure that you have the soil in good physical condition to encourage a strong root system.

When to sow
Mid-June to mid-July. It may, of course, be sown earlier but is not usually wanted as a summer vegetable.

How to sow
In drills 1 in (2·5 cm) deep and 18 in (45 cm) apart. Thin by stages to 6 in (15 cm). Protect from birds if necessary, as the seedlings are sweet and an unprotected row can disappear in 24 hours.

Time to germination
Ten days if the soil is moist. Germination is hastened if the seed is soaked for 12 hours before sowing, but in this case the soil must be moist when sowing and kept so until germination, otherwise the seed may start to shoot and then dry out and die.

Perpetual spinach

Season of use
Autumn, spring and early summer. In mild districts and under protection some pickings are possible throughout the winter.

Good varieties
No named varieties. Listed as Perpetual Spinach, Spinach Beet or Leaf Beet.

Special note
Keep picking young and tender leaves for use. Pick the old and tough ones too to encourage more leaves. When flower stems begin to appear in spring it is time to discard the row and prepare for a new one.

Sweet corn

Sweet corn likes a sunny, sheltered position. It is quite decorative and may be grown in groups in the shrub or herbaceous border if no other space is available.

Soil
Compost or manure during winter digging if possible. Complete fertilizer at the rate of 3 oz per sq yd (100 g per sq m) raked in 14 days before sowing or planting.

When to sow or plant
Sowing outdoors: early districts, May; late districts, first week of June. Under cloches: mid-April. In pots in the frame: mid-April, for planting out in May or June.

How to sow
In drills 1 in (3 cm) deep. Distance between rows: 18 in (45 cm). Final distance between plants 12 in (30 cm). Sow in groups of three seeds close together every 12 in (30 cm) reducing each to one good seedling. Sow in the frame in seed compost in small peat pots, two or three seeds per pot, and reduce to one. Grow in several short rows rather than one long one to improve fertilization by air-borne pollen which falls from the 'tassel' to be caught on the sticky 'silk' of the cobs.

Time to germination
14–21 days. Be prepared to protect seedlings from birds with black cotton or nylon netting as soon as they emerge. Harvest at the correct time, when juice squeezed out of the kernels is the consistency of thin cream and before it becomes solid and starchy.

Special note
In dry weather keep plants well watered and mulched with straw or compost in the weeks before formation of ears.

Season of use
Fresh: August to October. Freezer life: good condition for a year.

Good varieties
For the small garden: Golden Midget and Midget Hybrid, spaced 6–8 in (15–20 cm) apart. For larger plots: Silver Queen, Honey and Cream, Early Xtra Sweet.

Well-filled ears of sweet corn. The crop is easily spoiled by harvesting too late, when sugar in the kernels has been turned to starch.

Index

aphids, 20, 22, 34
artichokes,
 globe, 40
 Jerusalem, 11, 22, 51
asparagus, 23, 25, 39
asparagus peas, 37

beans, 11, 13
 broad, 10, 22, 23, 25, 34
 dwarf, 6, 10, 19, 23, 24, 35
 early 10
 runner, 6, 10, 16, 19, 23, 24, 38
beetroot, 10, 11, 14, 17, 19, 23, 25, 48
beet, seakale, 23, 60
blackfly, 20, 34
brassicas, 10, 11, 12, 13, 20, 21, 26–33
broad beans, 10, 22, 23, 25, 34
 longpod, 25
broccoli, sprouting, 10, 11, 22, 23, 25, 30, 32
Brussels sprouts, 11, 20, 22, 23, 25, 26

cabbage aphis, 20
cabbage caterpillars, 20
cabbage lettuce, 45
cabbage root fly, 21
cabbages, 11, 21, 22
 autumn, 22, 29
 spring, 10, 22, 24, 25, 33
 summer, 22, 23, 29
 winter, 10, 20, 22, 33
calabrese, 10, 11, 23, 24, 30
calendar, gardening, 22–5
cantaloup melon, 23, 59
carrot fly, 21, 49
carrots, 10, 11, 13, 14, 16, 17, 19, 21, 22, 23, 49
 stump-rooted, 6
caterpillars, 20
cauliflowers, 11, 21
 autumn 22, 27
 summer, 22, 23, 28
 winter, 22, 27
celeriac, 50
celery, 11, 22, 23, 24, 25, 41
celery, turnip-rooted (celeriac), 50
chicory, 42
cloches, 18–19
clubroot, 21
compost, 8
compost heap, making a, 9
corn, sweet, 11, 19, 23, 24, 63
cos lettuce, 45
courgettes, 23, 58
crops,
 brassica, 10, 11, 12, 13, 20, 21, 26–33
 caring for, 14–15
 miscellaneous, 10, 11, 57–63
 permanent, 39–40
 planning, 10

root, 10, 11, 17, 22, 48–56
 rotation of, 10–11
 salad, 11, 41–7
 successional, 10–11
cucumbers, 11
 indoor, 23
 outdoor or ridge, 23, 24, 43
cultivation,
 digging, 6–7
 manures and fertilizers, 8-9, 11
 mulching, 16
 sowing and planting, 12–13
 thinning, 14
 tools and equipment, 4–5
 watering, 16
 weed control, 14, 15
curly lettuce, 45

digging, 6–7
diseases, 20–1
dwarf beans, 6, 10, 19, 23, 24, 35
dwarf tomatoes, 23

endive, 44

fertilizers, 8-9
flea beetle, 21
frames, garden, 18, 19

garden peas, 19, 36
 early, 10, 22, 23, 36
 maincrop, 23, 36
 second early, 22
globe artichokes, 40
greens,
 autumn, 23
 winter, 22, 23, 24

harvesting, 17
humus, 8, 16

Jerusalem artichokes, 11, 22, 51

kale, 11, 23, 31

leaf lettuce, 45
leeks, 10, 11, 22, 24, 57
lettuce, 10, 13, 14, 16, 19, 22, 23, 24, 25, 45
liming, 9
long lettuce, 45
longpod broad beans, 25

mangetout, 37
manures, 8–9, 11
marrows, 11, 12, 13, 16, 17, 19, 23, 24, 58
melons, 23, 59
 cantaloup, 23, 59
mulching, 16

onions,
 bulb, 11, 17, 19, 22, 24, 52
 salad, 10, 11, 46

parsley, 22
parsnips, 11, 17, 22, 53

pea maggot, 21
peas, 11, 16, 21, 22
 asparagus, 37
 garden, 10, 19, 36
 round-seeded, 22, 25
 sugar, 37
perpetual spinach, 62
pests, 20–1
planning a vegetable plot, 10–11
planting, 12–13
potato blight, 21
potatoes, 6, 11, 17, 21, 22, 23, 54
 early, 10, 17, 22, 24, 54
 maincrop, 17, 54
 second early, 54
pumpkins, 17, 58

radishes, 10, 19, 21, 22, 23, 24, 46
root crops, 10, 11, 17, 22, 25, 48–56
root flies, 21
rotation of crops, 10–11
round lettuce, 45
round-seeded peas, 22, 25
round-seeded spinach, 10, 22, 61
runner beans, 6, 10, 16, 19, 23, 24, 38

salad crops, 11, 41–7
salad onions, 10, 11, 46
salsify, 11
seakale beet, 23, 60
seeds, 12–13, 25
shallots, 11, 17, 22, 24
slugs, 21
soils, 6
sowing, 12–13
spinach, 10, 11, 14, 16, 23
 perpetual, 62
 summer or round-seeded, 10, 22, 60
spinach beet, 10, 23, 62
spring cabbage, 10, 22, 24, 25, 33
sprouting broccoli,
 green (calabrese), 10, 11, 23, 24, 30
 white or purple, 10, 11, 23, 32
sprouts, Brussels, 11, 20, 22, 23, 25, 26
squashes, 11, 17, 23, 24, 58
 winter, 17
storage, 17
successional crops, 10–11
sugar peas, 37
summer spinach, 10, 22, 61
swedes, 11, 17, 21, 23, 55
sweet corn, 11, 19, 23, 24, 63

thinning, 14
tomatoes,
 dwarf, 23
 outdoor, 11, 12, 13, 19, 23, 24, 47
tools and equipment, 4–5
turnip-rooted celery (celeriac), 50
turnips, 10, 11, 14, 17, 21, 22, 23, 56

watering, 16
weed control, 14–15

64